Undisputed

The Greatest Heavyweight Boxers Go Head to Head

Bruce Anthony

Printed in the United Kingdom

Cover Art by Alejandro Colucci

Editing by Christie Erskine Editing

©Bruce Anthony, 2024

First edition

Dedication

For Mariya

Contents

Introduction

O n Saturday the 25th of February 1995, the boxing world witnessed a fight that would become infamous among fans, news outlets and critics of the sport. Held at the London Arena in London, England, the Dark Destroyer Nigel Benn faced off against the G-Man Gerald McClellan; a clash that saw two of the biggest punchers in the middleweight and super middleweight division square off in an epic barn burner of a fight that displayed both the beauty and brutality of boxing.

McClellan entered the fight as the bookmakers' favourite at 1/3 and was described as the Mike Tyson of the lower divisions. The American arrived to huge fanfare and interest, having come off the back of fourteen straight victories. This fight was seen as another opportunity to notch up a highlight reel KO against a well-known name.

McClellan's handlers considered Benn to be on the slide and were confidently predicting an impressive knockout win for their man. Unfortunately for them, Benn was bang up for the fight and hit just as hard with an astounding eighty-three percent KO ratio.

The fight began as predicted, and McClellan knocked Benn out of the ring within thirty-five seconds. What followed was a colossal back-and-forth battle filled with knockdowns, intensity, excitement and a late comeback from Benn that gave him the win in thrilling fashion.

Some accused McClellan of quitting, which is ridiculous and highlights the fickle nature of boxing fans and commentators. If anything, McClellan was nothing short of a warrior who fought until he had nothing left.

The fight was violent and tragic, with McClellan sadly suffering brain damage which left him blind and with hearing, memory and mobility issues. What these boxers put themselves through for our entertainment is incredible.

So why have I started with such a downbeat story?

Simply put, as a ten-year-old boy watching his first full boxing fight, I was enthralled. I had never seen such a spectacle, and once the fight was over I excitedly retold what happened to everyone who bothered to listen. Family, friends and random strangers were probably thinking, *Who's this weird kid babbling on about a boxing fight?*

On that day, I fell in love with the sport. In the following almost thirty years, I have followed the sport intensely, reading numerous books, staying up late to watch the big fights in Vegas or New York, and debating on online forums with random guys about how one fighter would easily beat another.

Putting this on paper does make me sound a bit sad, but when you are passionate about something you should always embrace it.

Thinking about fantasy fights between past greats and modern fighters has always fascinated me.

Some argue that sport has evolved too much and athletes from bygone eras just couldn't compete with modern greats. While it is true that sportsmen and women are physically bigger, faster and generally stronger than in previous eras – you only have to look at sports such as athletics or powerlifting to see that records set thirty plus years ago are now the average – but boxing is one of those unique sports where the physical isn't as important as the mental.

A famous quote by Georges St-Pierre illustrates this: "A fight is ten percent physical and ninety percent mental."

No matter how advanced training techniques have become, you can't put muscle on your chin, and you either can take a hard shot or you can't. Boxing matches are also twelve rounds now instead of fifteen, so naturally heavyweights can carry more muscle than they were able to when having to fight for another three rounds.

However, the biggest factor that normally determines the outcome of a fight is boxing skill or technique. And the fundamental training to be a great boxer is the same as it was nearly a hundred years ago: a combination of jump rope, speed bag, heavy bag, running and sparring. New things have been added here and there, but the basics are the basics, and they work.

A perfect example is Anthony Joshua, a great modern-day champion who hits as hard as anyone and is a big, strong guy at six feet six inches and 240 pounds.

Is AJ more skilled than Mike Tyson or Muhammad Ali? In short, no.

Is he faster than either? Again, no.

Does he hit harder? Probably not harder than Tyson, though he does have more power than Ali.

He doesn't have the chin or stamina of either fighter, and if he were to step into the ring with either I would be confident in betting that Tyson knocks him out in five, and Ali outboxes him similar to how Usyk did.

So, to summarise, past greats can absolutely stand up to the greats of today. In this book you will see many legends defeating fighters who came after them. You will also notice that size does play an important role in fights, as long as this isn't the only thing the boxer has in his favour.

We will start with a brief bio looking at each of the twenty fighters, including their stats, achievements, strengths and weaknesses. Once all combatants have entered the ring (or, in this case, the pages of this book) I will rank each fighter based on their achievements over their entire career.

The second half of the book will be a hypothetical league where each fighter goes against the other nineteen, including a simulation of how I believe those fights would have gone, resulting in a ranking system with a final decision on who the true GOAT is.

I will also give each fighter a personal rating for each of the key areas that make a great boxer: power, speed, chin, heart, stamina and ring IQ.

I hope you guys really enjoy this book. The feedback on some fights I've posted on forums has been overwhelmingly positive (aside from the one weirdo stalking my posts on Boxing Scene, but he shall remain nameless!).

Please bear in mind this is all subjective and everyone is entitled to their own opinions. With something of this nature there is no right or wrong, and this is all hypothetical. That said, this book will involve a close analysis of each fighter's career, strengths, weaknesses and performances against other fighters to come to the most accurate conclusion possible.

I have tried my best to stay unbiased and always focus on the data and information to hand when deciding winners, though I expect you to have your own opinions on how some of these tussles would have played out. At the end of the day, the main objective of this book is to shine a light on all these past greats and spark debate and interest in a sport we all love.

My hope is that, by reading this, you guys learn a thing or two and recognise these truly great boxers for the legacy they have left behind. I want to acknowledge the impact they have had not only on the sport of boxing, but the wider world.

If you are still reading this, you're probably feeling like I do before a big fight when the commentator rambles on to kill time. So, without further ado, the announcer is in the ring...

Ladies and gentlemen ... are you ready?

Boxing fans from around the world, I said: Are. You. Ready?

Let the ring walks begin!

Boxer Profiles

The fantastic thing about the heavyweight division is that there have been so many great fighters over the last hundred years. Naturally, that means that some have missed the cut.

It seems as though every decade a new great fighter emerges and establishes themselves as the best boxer in the division. Then as their career ends, someone else is there to claim the crown. On rare occasions, the old great fights the new young lion. Some examples of this include Joe Louis vs. Rocky Marciano (1951), Muhammad Ali vs. Larry Holmes (1980), Larry Holmes vs. Mike Tyson (1988) and Lennox Lewis vs. Vitali Klitschko (2003).

For the most part these fights are seen as a passing of the torch, however that isn't always the case, namely in the controversial match between Klitschko and Lewis, where Klitschko lost on cuts.

With over 3,000 heavyweight fighters in the history of the sport, it wasn't an easy task to create a shortlist of twenty for this book, and some great fighters have missed the cut. Some honourable omissions include Archie Moore, Bob Fitzsimmons, Jim Corbett, Ezzard Charles, Jersey Joe Walcott, Leon Spinks, Sam Longford and Max Baer, to name a few.

Only fighters that have ended their careers will be included, so current fighters at the time of writing who are still active – such as Tyson Fury, Anthony Joshua, Deontay Wilder and Oleksandr Usyk –unfortunately won't be included, as it is unfair to compare a fighter who has finished their career to someone who is midway through theirs. When the current generation retires, I can look at updating this book.

The twenty fighters I have featured in this book have left an indelible mark on the history of boxing. So, with gloves on and adrenaline pumping, let's step into the ring and dive into the achievements and careers of the twenty greatest heavyweights in boxing history to see who comes out on top.

Lights. Camera. Action!

Our first combatant to enter the arena is…

Evander Holyfield

Tale of the Tape

Prime age: 30

Fights: 57

Wins: 44

KOs: 29

Losses: 10

Draws: 2

KO percentage: 51%

Rounds boxed: 443

Height: 6 feet 2.5 inches

Weight: 217 pounds

Reach: 77.5 inches

Stance: Orthodox

Achievements

- Only four-time world heavyweight champion.
- Only fighter to win an undisputed championship in two weight classes.
- Olympic silver medallist.

Statistics

Power: 75

Speed: 85

Chin: 90

Heart: 100

Stamina: 90

Ring IQ: 90

Total: 530/600 = 88%

Our first fighter is the legendary Real Deal Evander Holyfield. Holyfield began his professional career in 1984 and quickly rose through the ranks, winning his first world championship in the cruiserweight division in 1986 before going on to become the undisputed cruiserweight champion.

He is possibly the greatest cruiserweight in history, with the other candidate for this accolade being Oleksandr Usyk.

After cleaning out the cruiserweight division he then moved up to the heavyweight ranks. He won his first world championship in that weight class in 1990, becoming the first fighter in history to win the undisputed title in two weight divisions (at the time of writing).

A true warrior who wasn't afraid to mix it up with anyone, Holyfield can only be respected and admired for his achievements. With a stellar resume that includes two wins over both Mike Tyson one win over Riddick Bowe; a draw and a close second fight with a prime Lennox Lewis; and wins against George Foreman, Larry Holmes, Buster Douglas, Michael Moorer, Ray Mercer, John Ruiz and Hasim Rahman rounding out his career.

Looking at his losses, the most glaring one is his loss to Michael Moorer. Holyfield suffered from health issues during the contest and Moorer put up a career-best performance. A rematch between the two showed the difference in class, with Holyfield avenging the loss.

His other major losses were to prime Riddick Bowe (twice) and Lennox Lewis (once), both of whom would beat the majority of fighters, and then some losses towards the tail end of his career to lesser opponents. Overall, he had an astonishing career.

Evander Holyfield was known for his aggressive and relentless style in the ring. He was a skilled boxer with a strong jab and powerful hooks and was also known for his exceptional footwork, which allowed him to move around the ring quickly and effectively.

But Holyfield's biggest strength was, by far, his heart and mental toughness. No fighter could ever intimidate him, and this speaks volumes, having shared a ring with some fearsome fighters like Tyson, Bowe, Foreman and Lewis.

Evander also possessed good fundamentals, combination punching, stamina, a solid chin, in-fighting and ring IQ.

He had two major weaknesses, the first being average power for a heavyweight – understandable considering he came up from cruiserweight and was therefore relatively undersized compared to other heavyweights. He also had a tendency to engage in wars when he could have relied on his skills, however this is what made Holyfield such a great fighter and a formidable opponent.

Floyd Patterson

Tale of the Tape

Prime age: 25

Fights: 64

Wins: 55

KOs: 40

Losses: 8

Draws: 1

KO percentage: 63%

Rounds boxed: 421

Height: 5 feet 11 inches

Weight: 188 pounds

Reach: 69.5 inches

Stance: Orthodox

Achievements

- Two-time world heavyweight champion.
- Youngest world heavyweight champion at the time (at twenty-one years old).
- Olympic gold medallist.

Statistics

Power: 80

Speed: 97

Chin: 70

Heart: 85

Stamina: 90

Ring IQ: 85

Total: 507/600 = 85%

Hopping into the arena now is the great Floyd Patterson, known as the "Gentleman of Boxing" or, as Muhammed Ali used to call him, "the Rabbit".

Born on the 4th of January 1935, in Waco, North Carolina, Patterson had an illustrious career that spanned two decades from 1952 to 1972. In 1956, at the age of twenty-one, he became the youngest world heavyweight champion in history when he defeated Archie Moore.

Floyd Patterson was known for his unique fighting style that combined speed, agility and power. He was a master of the peek-a-boo technique, which was popularised by his trainer Cus D'Amato. This involved keeping the hands high in front of the face, with the elbows tucked in, providing excellent protection while allowing for quick counterpunching.

Patterson's footwork was also exceptional, as he constantly moved in and out of range, making it difficult for his opponents to land clean punches. His speed and agility allowed him to dart in and out, delivering lightning-fast combinations and then quickly evading his opponent's counterattacks.

Patterson's career was marked by several notable fights, including famous bouts against Ingemar Johansson. The two fighters engaged in a trilogy of fights between 1959 and 1961, with Johansson emerging victorious in the first, but Patterson winning the second and third fights. These fights captivated the boxing world and showcased Patterson's resilience and determination.

Unfortunately, Patterson was quite protected by Cus, who made sure to avoid big punchers. It was only after Patterson fired Cus that he started taking on the big challenges and tough fights. It is a shame that he never fought heavy hitters such as Zora Folley or Cleveland Williams, and by the time he did fight elite fighters such as Sonny Liston or Muhammad Ali, he was soundly beaten.

His best wins include matches against Archie Moore, George Chuvalo, Oscar Bonavena, Ingemar Johansson (twice) and Henry Cooper, but with losses to Johansson, Sonny Liston (twice), Muhammad Ali (twice) and Jerry Quarry, Patterson just about makes it onto this list.

George Foreman

Tale of the Tape

Prime age: 24

Fights: 81

Wins: 76

KOs: 68

Losses: 5

Draws: 0

KO percentage: 84%

Rounds boxed: 349

Height: 6 feet 4 inches

Weight: 220 pounds

Reach: 79 inches

Stance: Orthodox

Achievements

- Two-time world heavyweight champion.
- Oldest world heavyweight champion at forty-five years of age.
- Olympic gold medallist.
- Competed successfully in the two golden eras of heavyweight boxing: the seventies and nineties.

Statistics

Power: 100

Speed: 80

Chin: 95

Heart: 85

Stamina: 70

Ring IQ: 80

Total: 510/600 = 85%

Coming down to the ring now is none other than George Foreman. Foreman first rose to prominence in the late 1960s and early 1970s after winning a gold medal at the 1968 Olympics.

He quickly gained a reputation as a fearsome puncher, with his devastating right hand earning him the nickname "Big George". Foreman was known for his powerful punching ability and his imposing physical presence in the ring, standing at six feet four inches and weighing over 210 pounds.

Foreman made a stunning comeback to boxing in 1987, at the age of thirty-eight. He won his second world heavyweight title in 1994, at the age of forty-five, making him the oldest world heavyweight champion in history.

Foreman's fighting style was heavily influenced by his physical attributes. He was a large and powerful man, and his size and strength allowed him to dominate and overwhelm his opponents in the ring. He often used his weight to lean on foes and wear them down.

He was known for his ability to deliver devastating blows with both hands and for throwing punches from unorthodox angles, which made them difficult to defend against. He could also take a punch and keep fighting, making him a formidable opponent in the ring.

Despite his aggressive style, Foreman was also a smart fighter who was able to read his opponents, understand their styles and weaknesses and adjust his strategy accordingly, which allowed him to win fights against opponents who were technically superior to him.

He was also a patient fighter who was willing to wait for the right moment to strike, which made him a dangerous opponent in the ring.

Looking at Foreman's resume, one can only marvel at the list of all-time greats he shared a ring with in two different eras.

During the seventies he had two devastating wins over Joe Frazier and one over Ken Norton, Ron Lyle and George Chuvalo. He had a KO loss to Muhammad Ali and a decision loss to Jimmy Young, when George was suffering from heatstroke due to the humidity.

Looking at this part of George's career alone, you have to rank him highly in the all-time great discussion. Combined with what he did in his comeback, you can make an argument for him being the best ever.

Foreman's comeback, starting at age thirty-eight, strung together twenty-four straight wins, including against some decent names like Gerry Cooney and Dwight Muhammed Qawi. Going up against a prime Holyfield and putting on a strong performance at forty-two years old shows how great a fighter Foreman was.

His other later fights demonstrate his toughness and ring IQ: a loss to Michael Morrison, who used his speed and footwork to outbox Foreman; a win over Lou Savarese; a majority decision loss to

Shannon Briggs; and the highlight of his comeback, a knockout victory over Michael Moorer to become the oldest and one of the greatest heavyweights in history.

Gene Tunney

Tale of the Tape

Prime age: 30

Fights: 88

Wins: 82

KOs: 49

Losses: 1

Draws: 4

KO percentage: 56%

Rounds boxed: 589

Height: 6 feet

Weight: 190 pounds

Reach: 76 inches

Stance: Orthodox

Achievements

- World heavyweight champion.
- Only one loss (which was later avenged) among eighty-eight fights.
- Undefeated as a heavyweight.

Statistics

Power: 80

Speed: 85

Chin: 95

Heart: 90

Stamina: 100

Ring IQ: 95

Total: 545/600 = 91%

Gene Tunney, born on the 25th of May 1897, was an American professional boxer who competed from 1915 to 1928. He held the world heavyweight title from 1926 to 1928, and the American light heavyweight title twice between 1922 and 1923.

Tunney had a five-fight light heavyweight rivalry with Harry Greb, in which he won three, drew once and lost once. However, he is best remembered for his two fights with Jack Dempsey. He won both matches, the first in 1926 and the second in 1927. The second fight is still remembered as the "Long Count Fight", where Tunney was given extra time to recover from a knockdown, which led to a controversial win.

Known as "the Fighting Marine", Tunney was a great technical fighter. Using defensive skills and movement, he was able to confuse and out-box some really great fighters. Tunney held his hands low, which he believed gave him added power. However, with only a fifty-six percent knockout ratio, he clearly wasn't a big puncher.

Any fighter of a similar size or smaller would be considered the underdog against Tunney, however at only six feet tall and 190 pounds, he would struggle against other all-time great fighters who were naturally bigger.

Being one of only two boxers on this list to be undefeated at heavyweight and his only loss coming to Harry Greb (one of the greatest fighters of all time) surely has to put Gene Tunney up there with some of the all-time greats.

Jack Dempsey

Tale of the Tape

Prime age: 24

Fights: 85

Wins: 68

KOs: 53

Losses: 6

Draws: 9

KO percentage: 62%

Rounds boxed: 335

Height: 6 feet 1 inch

Weight: 188 pounds

Reach: 73 inches

Stance: Orthodox

Achievements

- World heavyweight champion.
- Had close to a seven-year title reign.
- Holds record for highest KO to win ratio in world title fights, at eighty-five percent.

Statistics

Power: 90

Speed: 85

Chin: 90

Heart: 90

Stamina: 95

Ring IQ: 80

Total: 530/600 = 88%

The Manassa Mauler was a ferocious fighter, with dynamite in both hands and a killer instinct that rivalled any great.

Jack Dempsey was a truly special fighter. His win over Jess Willard has to be the most one-sided utter destruction of a champion in history. Dempsey's trainer informed him before the fight that he had bet his purse on a knockout win. This was all an incensed Dempsey needed to hear. He went on to lay what was probably the worst beat-down ever given to a much larger opponent.

At six feet six inches, Willard towered over Dempsey. But that didn't matter; he was out for blood. He knocked Willard down seven times in the first round (at a time when you could stand over your fallen opponent), then proceeded to break Willard's jaw and ribs, cause multiple facial fractures and hearing loss in one ear.

I guess you have to be one devastating fighter for Mike Tyson to consider you his hero.

Dempsey's resume is quite lacking when it comes to defeating truly great fighters, with his two stand-out wins coming via Jess Willard and Jack Sharkey, neither the greatest fighter. Also, his two losses to Gene Tunney, who completely outboxed him, definitely count against him.

At only six feet one and 188 pounds he would struggle against any technical fighter the same size or bigger than himself. However, with an iron will and TNT in both fists, Dempsey would be trouble for any boxer.

Jack Johnson

Tale of the Tape

Prime age: 32

Fights: 95

Wins: 72

KOs: 38

Losses: 11

Draws: 11

KO percentage: 40%

Rounds boxed: 858

Height: 6 feet 0.5 inches

Weight: 209 pounds

Reach: 74 inches

Stance: Orthodox

Achievements

- First African American heavyweight champion.
- Seven-year title reign.

Statistics

Power: 70

Speed: 80

Chin: 80

Heart: 85

Stamina: 100

Ring IQ: 90

Total: 505/600 = 84%

Next into the arena is none other than the Galveston Giant Jack Johnson.

Johnson was an American boxer with the unique distinction of being the first African American to become the world heavyweight champion. He held the title from 1908 to 1915, during a time of extreme racial tension in the United States. Johnson's success in the ring challenged the prevailing racial stereotypes of the time, and he faced significant backlash from both the media and the public.

Johnson's fighting style was heavily influenced by his background in dance. He was known for his graceful movements and fluid footwork, which allowed him to move around the ring with ease.

Johnson was also a master of feints and fakes, often using these techniques to set up his opponents for powerful counterpunches. He was a strategic fighter, always looking for weaknesses in his opponents' defences and exploiting them to his advantage.

Johnson's fighting style was controversial at the time, as it went against the popular boxing style of the era. He was criticised for his defensive tactics and accused of prolonging fights in order to entertain the crowd. However, Johnson's style proved to be highly effective with him becoming the best heavyweight in the world and one of the all-time greats.

His resume is very strong, having fought ninety-five times and amassing an astonishing 858 rounds boxed – by far the most experience in the ring compared to any other heavyweight in this book. (Please bear in mind that fights back then had an unimaginable number of rounds, and if both fighters were still standing at the end, the fight was declared a draw.)

Big wins over Sam Langford, Bob Fitzsimmons and Jim Jeffries round out a truly historic and trailblazing career. Johnson was one of the most courageous fighters to have ever lived.

Jim Jeffries

Tale of the Tape

Prime age: 25

Fights: 24

Wins: 19

KOs: 16

Losses: 1

Draws: 2

KO percentage: 60%

Rounds boxed: 222

Height: 6 feet

Weight: 225 pounds

Reach: 76.5 inches

Stance: Orthodox

Achievements

- World heavyweight champion.
- Only loss was to Jack Johnson long after retirement.

Statistics

Power: 80

Speed: 80

Chin: 90

Heart: 85

Stamina: 100

Ring IQ: 80

Total: 515/600 = 86%

Our next fighter is the Boilermaker, Jim Jeffries. Jeffries was a professional boxer who competed from 1896 to 1905. He is best known for his reign as the heavyweight champion from 1899 to 1904.

Known for his aggressive and powerful style of fighting, Jeffries was a skilled puncher who knocked out many of his opponents. He was also known for his strong chin, which allowed him to take a lot of punishment in the ring.

Jeffries was famous for his use of the left jab, which enabled him to set up his powerful overhand right. Known for his ability to fight on the inside, he would use his strength and power to wear down opponents. Jeffries was a master at cutting off the ring and trapping his rivals in the corners where he could unleash his powerful punches.

The most notable wins of his career include James J. Corbett (twice), Bob Fitzsimmons (twice) and Tom Sharkey.

With only twenty-four fights, Jeffries has the lowest number of contests on this list by quite some margin. He retired from boxing in 1905, but with mounting pressure from fans and news outlets he made the unwise decision to come out of retirement in 1910 to fight Jack Johnson, hoping to restore lost pride to the white race.

Jeffries was soundly defeated in the fight – the only loss of his career – which was seen as a major turning point in the history of boxing. By 1910, Jeffries' style of fighting was viewed as outdated, and this fight helped usher in a new era of boxing where speed and agility were more important than brute strength.

Joe Frazier

Tale of the Tape

Prime age: 27

Fights: 37

Wins: 32

KOs: 27

Losses: 4

Draws: 1

KO percentage: 73%

Rounds boxed: 212

Height: 5 feet 11 inches

Weight: 205 pounds

Reach: 73.5 inches

Stance: Orthodox

Achievements

- World heavyweight champion.
- Olympic gold medallist.
- Holds perhaps the single greatest win in heavyweight boxing over Muhammad Ali in the *Fight of the Century*.

Statistics

Power: 85

Speed: 85

Chin: 85

Heart: 100

Stamina: 100

Ring IQ: 85

Total: 540/600 = 90%

Our next fighter is none other than Smokin' Joe Frazier. A real tough, gritty fighter with the heart of a lion and a fearlessness rarely seen.

Born on the 12th of January 1944, in Beaufort, South Carolina, his early life was marked by poverty and hardship as the youngest of twelve children. Frazier developed an interest in boxing at a young age. He fashioned a homemade punching bag out of burlap sacks stuffed with moss and leaves, which he hung on a tree. He began his boxing training in earnest after moving to Philadelphia.

In the early 1960s, Frazier emerged as a promising heavyweight boxer. He won the Middle Atlantic Golden Gloves heavyweight championship three times, as well as an Olympic gold medal in the 1964 games in Tokyo, Japan.

Fighting with a mauling crab-like style and having possibly the greatest left hook in heavyweight history, Frazier was one hell of a fighter. His bob and weave style enabled him to get up close to let his punches go, with great wins over Joe Bugner, Buster Mathis, Jimmy Ellis, Oscar Bonavena and Jerry Quarry displaying how effective the style could be.

He also holds perhaps the greatest win in heavyweight history with his decision victory over Muhammad Ali in the *Fight of the Century*.

Frazier did have some obvious weaknesses. His style was tailor-made for big punchers like George Foreman, which was evidenced in Kingston, Jamaica when Frazier was knocked out in two rounds by Big George. Relying on taking a shot to give a shot against big hitters known for their punching power isn't always the smartest of strategies.

Frazier's chin also wasn't the strongest, and being five feet eleven, he wasn't the biggest either. He would struggle against much larger opponents who could hit hard.

Nonetheless, Frazier was a true warrior of the sport. With no quit in him, Frazier most likely would have gone undefeated in most other eras, however when your two main contemporaries are Muhammad Ali and George Foreman, that's almost an impossibility.

Frazier, Ali, Foreman and Ken Norton all helped to create the best era in heavyweight boxing, with each making the other greater.

Joe Louis

Tale of the Tape

Prime age: 24

Fights: 69

Wins: 66

KOs: 52

Losses: 3

Draws: 0

KO percentage: 75%

Rounds boxed: 417

Height: 6 feet 2 inches

Weight: 194 pounds

Reach: 76 inches

Stance: Orthodox

Achievements

- World heavyweight champion.
- Twelve-year reign as champion.
- Twenty-five consecutive title defences, a record which still stands today across all weight divisions.

Statistics

Power: 92

Speed: 85

Chin: 80

Heart: 95

Stamina: 100

Ring IQ: 85

Total: 537/600 = 90%

Next up is the Brown Bomber, Joe Louis. Born on the 13th of May 1914, in Lafayette, Alabama, Louis was one of the greatest heavyweights in the history of the sport. If you ask any boxing historian to rank the greatest heavyweight fighters, he would be in pretty much everyone's top three, even topping quite a few lists.

Louis was the son of sharecroppers and the grandson of slaves, who moved with his family to Detroit, Michigan at the age of twelve. He took up boxing as a teenager at a local youth recreation centre.

In his amateur career, Louis won fifty out of fifty-four matches, with forty-three knockouts. He turned professional in 1934 and quickly rose through the ranks with a series of impressive victories.

Possessing great hand speed, knockout power, stamina and combination punching, Louis would give any heavyweight a tough night's work. With impressive wins over Primo Carnera, Max Baer, Jack Sharkey, Max Schmeling and Jersey Joe Walcott (twice), Louis beat pretty much all the top fighters of his era.

A look at his career wouldn't be complete without touching on his two historic fights with Max Schmeling.

The first was a perfect example of a fighter studying his opponent's weak points and exploiting them to maximum advantage. Schmeling noticed that after Louis threw a left jab, rather than bringing his hand back up to his chin, he let it stay low. This presented an opening for the right cross counter. After twelve long and brutal rounds, Schmeling was able to knockout Louis in what has to be one of the greatest wins in heavyweight history.

The rematch between the two rivals ended in just as conclusive fashion, with Louis knocking out Schmeling in round one.

We also have to look at Louis' other fight against an all-time great, Rocky Marciano. By October 1951, Louis was thirty-seven years old and no longer the fighter he had been in his twenties, however he was forced to continue boxing due to financial reasons.

At the start of the fight he showed glimpses of his old self, and still lasted until the eighth round. However, as the fight wore on, Rocky's relentless pressure and body punching was too much for him. A prime Louis, with his bigger size, better boxing ability and sheer power would probably have been too much for Marciano to handle.

Ken Norton

Tale of the Tape

Prime age: 30

Fights: 50

Wins: 42

KOs: 33

Losses: 7

Draws: 1

KO percentage: 66%

Rounds boxed: 315

Height: 6 feet 3 inches

Weight: 210 pounds

Reach: 80 inches

Stance: Orthodox

Achievements

- World heavyweight champion.

Statistics

Power: 80

Speed: 80

Chin: 70

Heart: 90

Stamina: 100

Ring IQ: 80

Total: 500/600 = 83%

Entering the arena now is the Black Hercules, Ken Norton. Norton was an American professional boxer born on the 9th of August 1943 in Jacksonville, Illinois. He had a successful amateur career before turning professional, winning the National AAU heavyweight title in 1967 and retiring in 1981.

He was known for his durability in the ring, taking on some of the toughest opponents of his era. Norton was also known for his physical strength, muscular build and for his ability to go the distance in fights. His endurance enabled him to maintain a high level of performance throughout the duration of a fight, often outlasting his opponents in terms of stamina and energy.

Norton had a unique boxing style, utilising a cross-arm defence and a strong jab. One notable aspect of Norton's fighting style was his strong defensive skills. He had a knack for blocking and parrying punches and using clever footwork to evade his opponents' attacks, making it difficult for his opponents to land clean shots on him. His defensive prowess allowed him to frustrate his opponents and minimise the damage he took during fights.

Norton's first fight against Muhammad Ali on the 31st of March 1973 was a significant upset. Norton broke Ali's jaw in the early rounds and won the fight by split decision. The rematch between Norton and Ali took place on the 10th of September 1973, and Ali won by split decision. They then had a third and final fight on the 28th of September 1976, which Ali won by unanimous decision.

A standout win over Ali in their first fight was the highlight of Norton's career, alongside a big win over Jerry Quarry. A devastating KO loss to George Foreman in two rounds and another two losses to Ali followed (though the third fight can be argued in his favour, as watching the fight back, Ali was clearly clowning around several times). A very close loss to a prime Larry Holmes and two KO losses to Earnie Shavers and Gerry Cooney round out a successful career for a warrior, who found himself in the middle of the greatest era in the heavyweight division.

Larry Holmes

Tale of the Tape

Prime age: 31

Fights: 75

Wins: 69

KOs: 44

Losses: 6

Draws: 0

KO percentage: 59%

Rounds boxed: 579

Height: 6 feet 3 inches

Weight: 215 pounds

Reach: 81 inches

Stance: Orthodox

Achievements

- Seven-year reign as world heavyweight champion.
- Forty-eight fights undefeated.
- Handed Muhammad Ali the only stoppage loss of his career.

Statistics

Power: 80

Speed: 85

Chin: 90

Heart: 90

Stamina: 90

Ring IQ: 90

Total: 525/600 = 87.5%

Our next fighter is none other than the Easton Assassin, Larry Holmes. Holmes began his professional career in 1973, and he quickly established himself as a formidable fighter.

He won his first forty-eight fights and became the WBC heavyweight champion in 1978 after defeating Ken Norton in one of the greatest heavyweight fights in history, with victories over notable opponents such as Muhammad Ali, Ken Norton and Earnie Shavers. He held the WBC heavyweight title from 1978 to 1983 and the IBF heavyweight title from 1983 to 1985.

Unfortunately, Holmes was never the most popular champion, probably due to having the misfortune of coming after the great Ali and before Iron Mike Tyson, two of the most exciting and charismatic champions to have existed.

However, we are not here to review popularity, but rather each fighter's achievements and abilities in the squared circle. From that perspective, Holmes can hold his own against pretty much anyone.

Good wins over Ken Norton, Earnie Shavers (twice), Muhammad Ali (albeit faded), Trevor Berbick, Leon Spinks and Gerry Cooney and losses to great fighters such as Leon Spinks (twice), Mike Tyson and Evander Holyfield round out a strong resume.

The biggest issue with Holmes' career is the lack of a legacy-defining win over an all-time great fighter in his prime – the closest being a hard-fought fight with Norton.

Larry Holmes was known for his excellent jab, which he used to control the distance and pace of his fights. He had a long reach and used it to keep his opponents at bay, making it difficult for them to land punches.

Holmes was also a master of the counterpunch, often catching his opponents off guard with quick and powerful shots. Holmes was also a skilled defensive fighter, often slipping and dodging punches effortlessly.

Despite being a big and strong heavyweight, Holmes was also known for his agility and footwork. He was able to move around the ring with ease, making it difficult for his opponents to corner him.

His biggest strengths were his fantastic left jab – arguably the best in history – solid fundamentals, fast hands and feet and a great heart. His only real weakness was his lack of significant power, with only a fifty-nine percent KO ratio.

Lennox Lewis

Tale of the Tape

Prime age: 36

Fights: 44

Wins: 41

KOs: 32

Losses: 2

Draws: 1

KO percentage: 72%

Rounds boxed: 225

Height: 6 feet 5 inches

Weight: 249 pounds

Reach: 84 inches

Stance: Orthodox

Achievements

- Three-time world heavyweight champion.
- Two-time lineal world heavyweight champion.
- Undisputed heavyweight champion
- Olympic gold medallist.
- Defeated every man he stepped into the ring with.

Statistics

Power: 95

Speed: 80

Chin: 80

Heart: 95

Stamina: 90

Ring IQ: 100

Total: 540/600 = 90%

Our next fighter is none other than the Lion himself, Lennox Lewis.

Standing at six feet five and weighing 249 pounds, Lewis is the first of the super heavyweights on this list – a formidable fighter with an outstanding jab, uppercut and overhand right that could knock anyone out if landed clean.

The two weaknesses for Lewis are his average chin and losing to two mediocre fighters in Oliver McCall and Hasim Rahman. Even though he avenged both defeats in spectacular fashion, the fact that he suffered such dreadful defeats has to be factored in when considering his greatness.

Furthermore, Lewis' signature wins were a shot Tyson and past-his-prime Holyfield. Though Lewis won both fights against Evander Holyfield, the second fight was very close, and it can be argued that the Holyfield from the Bowe fights could have beaten him.

It is a real shame for the sport that a Lewis vs. Bowe fight never happened, as both were in their primes and this would have told us a lot about who the best fighter of the nineties was.

However, even taking these points into consideration, Lewis still put together a great resume filled with top names such as Frank Bruno, Tony Tucker, Tommy Morrison, Shannon Briggs, David Tua, Ray Mercer, Donovan Ruddock and Vitali Klitschko (the latter being his best win, in my opinion).

To this day there is still a lot of controversy surrounding the fight with Klitschko. Klitschko was clearly ahead at the time of the stoppage and Lewis looked completely exhausted. It can be argued a rematch should have happened. However, Lewis' ring IQ and experience was what got him through. A fight can end in the following ways: KO, TKO, points win, corner throws in the towel or doctor stoppage due to cuts/injury. Lewis exploited a vulnerability he noticed by targeting the cuts on the left side of Vitali's face. In doing so, he gave the officials no choice but to call an end to proceedings.

As fans we all would have loved the fight to continue and Klitschko clearly wanted to, however a fighter needs to be protected from himself and if the fight had continued it could have caused some serious permanent damage.

If an out-of-shape Lewis can tear up Klitschko's face in such a way, what could a prime, in shape and focused Lewis have done?

Lewis is easily one of the greatest heavyweights in history. With his strength, size and heart he is undoubtedly one of the more difficult fighters to go up against on this list. Some would say he is the favourite and given his attributes it would be hard to argue against this.

Max Schmeling

Tale of the Tape

Prime age: 31

Fights: 70

Wins: 56

KOs: 40

Losses: 10

Draws: 4

KO percentage: 57%

Rounds boxed: 479

Height: 6 feet 1 inch

Weight: 192 pounds

Reach: 76 inches

Stance: Orthodox

Achievements

- World heavyweight champion.
- Only boxer to win world heavyweight title on a foul.
- Holds one of the greatest wins in heavyweight history with his victory over a prime Joe Louis.

Statistics

Power: 85

Speed: 75

Chin: 75

Heart: 85

Stamina: 90

Ring IQ: 85

Total: 495/600 = 83%

Our next fighter is the Black Uhlan of the Rhine, Max Schmeling. Born on the 28th of September 1905 in Klein Luckow, Germany, Schmeling started his boxing career in 1924 and quickly rose through the ranks, becoming the German heavyweight champion in 1928. He gained international fame when he defeated Jack Sharkey in 1930 to become the world heavyweight champion.

Schmeling was known for his powerful right hand and his ability to counterpunch effectively. His boxing style was characterised by his technical skills, footwork and strategic approach to the sport. He was known for his disciplined training and dedication to boxing, which contributed to his success in the ring.

Schmeling's main weaknesses were his slow foot and hand speed and average power, as well as being slightly undersized in comparison to some other fighters on this list.

One of Max Schmeling's most notable fights was against Joe Louis in 1936. At the time, Louis was an up-and-coming boxer and was considered a rising star in the heavyweight division. Schmeling, however, managed to defeat Louis in a surprising upset, knocking him out in the twelfth round. This victory made Schmeling a national hero in Germany and propelled him to international fame.

The rematch between Schmeling and Louis took place in 1938 and was highly anticipated. Louis was determined to avenge his previous loss, and the fight ended with Louis knocking out Schmeling in the first round.

Schmeling's two biggest wins were against Joe Louis and Jack Sharkey. He also suffered losses to the same two fighters, as well as Max Baer. With ten losses and his two biggest wins being avenged, it can be argued that Max overachieved for a fighter of his ability, or perhaps he simply just wasn't quite as good as an all-time great like Louis.

That said, Schmeling's legacy extends beyond his accomplishments in the ring; he is remembered as a respected figure both inside and outside the boxing world.

Mike Tyson

Tale of the Tape

Prime age: 21

Fights: 58

Wins: 50

KOs: 44

Losses: 6

Draws: 0

KO percentage: 76%

Rounds boxed: 215

Height: 5 feet 10 inches

Weight: 218 pounds

Reach: 71 inches

Stance: Orthodox

Achievements

- Youngest world heavyweight champion in history at twenty years and four months old.
- First heavyweight boxer to hold WBA, WBC and IBF titles and unify them in succession.
- Two-time world heavyweight champion.

Statistics

Power: 95

Speed: 95

Chin: 90

Heart: 70

Stamina: 85

Ring IQ: 85

Total: 520/600 = 87%

Now coming down the aisle, looking to uppercut someone's head clean off, is Kid Dynamite – Iron Mike Tyson.

Tyson burst onto the boxing scene in the 1980s and quickly became one of the most feared fighters in the world. He won his first nineteen fights by knockout and became the youngest heavyweight champion in history at the age of twenty.

Tyson's fighting style was heavily influenced by his trainer, Cus D'Amato, who taught him to be a peek-a-boo fighter. This style involved keeping the hands high to protect the face and using quick head movements to avoid punches. Tyson was also known for his incredible speed and reflexes, which allowed him to slip punches and counter with brutal hooks and uppercuts.

Tyson was known for his incredible power and his aggressive, relentless style. He would often charge at his opponents, throwing powerful punches and looking to end the fight quickly. Tyson was also a skilled inside fighter, and he was able to use his head movement and footwork to get in close to his opponents and deliver punishing blows.

Overall, Tyson's fighting style was characterised by his incredible power, speed and aggression. He was a fearsome opponent who struck fear into the hearts of his opponents, and he remains one of the most iconic boxers of all time.

Analysing his record is not only impressive but also makes you wonder *what if?* What if Tyson hadn't partnered with Don King? Or hadn't spent three years in prison? Or if the heavyweight division in the eighties was as strong as it was in the seventies and nineties.

Tyson cut through the division like a buzz saw during the eighties, amassing impressive wins over Trevor Berbick, Tony Tucker, Larry Holmes (underprepared and past his best), Michael Spinks and Frank Bruno.

By the end of the decade, Mike was clearly the best in the division and had unified all the major belts. However, cracks had already started to appear, with him neglecting training and becoming easily distracted by outside influences.

All of this came to a head with the biggest upset in boxing history when Tyson was stopped by a thousand-to-one rank outsider, Buster Douglas. The loss to Douglas was a perfect storm of Tyson not taking the opponent seriously, his corner not being able to deal with his left eye swelling, outside personal issues and Douglas boxing the fight of his life.

Tyson did bounce back with two wins over Donovan Razor Ruddock, however he was then incarcerated for three years, eventually making his return to the ring in 1995. During this time other great fighters such as Evander Holyfield, Riddick Bowe and Lennox Lewis emerged.

When they finally fought, Holyfield clearly showed who the better boxer was and dominated Tyson with a TKO in the first fight. In the second, Tyson knew he would lose and intentionally got himself disqualified.

Decent wins over Frank Bruno, Andrew Golota and Lou Savarese showed that he wasn't completely washed up, however Tyson was completely outclassed and KO'd by Lennox Lewis. A couple of losses at the end of his career sum up an unfortunate end to a spectacular career.

Muhammad Ali

Tale of the Tape

Prime age: 24

Fights: 61

Wins: 56

KOs: 37

Losses: 5

Draws: 0

KO percentage: 60%

Rounds boxed: 548

Height: 6 feet 3 inches

Weight: 214 pounds

Reach: 78 inches

Stance: Orthodox

Achievements

- First ever three-time world heavyweight champion.
- Olympic gold medallist.
- National Golden Gloves light heavyweight champion.
- Fought and defeated more all-time great fighters on this list than any other heavyweight.

Statistics

Power: 80

Speed: 100

Chin: 95

Heart: 100

Stamina: 100

Ring IQ: 100

Total: 575/600 = 96%

Entering the arena now is none other than Muhammad Ali. Known as "the Greatest", he truly was a phenomenal fighter. Blessed with blurring hand and foot speed, reflexes like a cat, stamina, strong ring IQ and a great chin with a sprinkle of bulletproof confidence, Ali is truly a one-of-a-kind fighter.

It could be argued his achievements outside of the ring were even greater than what he accomplished inside it, however we are here to analyse his in-ring performances.

No fighter on this list has fought as many other all-time great fighters as Ali, with wins over Sonny Liston, Floyd Patterson, Joe Frazier, George Foreman and Ken Norton. Combining these wins with a bunch of other victories over high-calibre fighters such as Archie Moore, Henry Cooper, George Chuvalo, Zora Folley, Ron Lyle and Joe Bugner, Ali easily has the deepest and strongest resume in heavyweight boxing history.

The only two blemishes on his record that were not avenged were early eighties fights against Larry Holmes and Trevor Berbick, however at this point he should have long been retired.

To fight killers like prime Liston and Foreman – who were known to intimidate their opponents into submission – shows incredible talent, toughness, boxing ability and courage.

It is hard to think of any fighter who would be favourite against a prime Ali; maybe Lennox Lewis, Riddick Bowe or possibly Tyson Fury, but no one else comes to mind. If aliens were to come to earth and challenge humans to a boxing fight, allowing us to select any fighter in their prime from the history of boxing, the general consensus would be to put Ali forward.

Ali's first main weakness was his susceptibility to the left hook, which he was put down with on numerous occasions. However, with a very strong chin this is slightly negated, and he was never stopped – aside from his fight with Holmes when he was way past his prime.

His second weakness was that, against lesser opponents, he had a tendency to clown around and not take them seriously. Ali was a bookies' nightmare since he would intentionally carry a fighter to the round he predicted he would finish them in.

In his toughest fights against Liston, Frazier and Foreman, Ali was one hundred percent focused, but that's not to say he didn't employ his legendary mind games to give him the edge, whether pre-fight or during.

From a conventional perspective, Ali held his hands low and pulled his head back from punches rather than blocking them. For a young Ali this wasn't an issue and actually allowed him to capitalise on his opponent's openings easier, however as he aged and his reflexes slowed, he did take one too many shots to the head. Unfortunately, this did end up contributing to his illness.

It is an honour to have such an amazing boxer on this list and I can't wait to see the performances he strings together.

Riddick Bowe

Tale of the Tape

Prime age: 25

Fights: 45

Wins: 43

KOs: 33

Losses: 1

Draws: 0

KO percentage: 73%

Rounds boxed: 195

Height: 6 feet 5 inches

Weight: 235 pounds

Reach: 81 inches

Stance: Orthodox

- Achievements
- Two-time world heavyweight champion.
- The first boxer in history to win all four sanctioning body belts at heavyweight: WBA, WBO, WBC and IBF.
- Olympic silver medallist.
- Only one loss, to Evander Holyfield.

Statistics

Power: 90

Speed: 80

Chin: 90

Heart: 90

Stamina: 90

Ring IQ: 90

Total: 530/600 = 88%

Known as "Big Daddy Bowe", Riddick Lamont Bowe was born on the 10th of August 1967, in Brooklyn, New York. He grew up in the Brownsville area of Brooklyn and began boxing at the age of thirteen. He had a successful amateur career, winning the New York Golden Gloves tournaments in 1985 and 1986.

Bowe's career was marked by relatively few notable fights, the highlights being his trilogy with Evander Holyfield. Their first fight in 1992 – where Bowe won by unanimous decision to become the undisputed champion – was named Fight of the Year by *Ring Magazine*. Holyfield won the rematch in 1993 via a razor-close decision, and Bowe won the third and final fight with a TKO in the eighth round. Some decent wins over Herbie Hide and Andrew Golota round out a pretty thin resume.

Never having shared a ring in the pro ranks with his Brooklyn contemporary Mike Tyson does hurt his legacy. As does his act of throwing the WBC belt into the trash rather than facing Lennox Lewis. (It has to be noted that the fight between Bowe and Lewis was later signed, however Lewis suffered a shock KO to Oliver McCall, which shelved the fight.)

Riddick Bowe was known for his aggressive and powerful fighting style. He was a skilled boxer with a strong jab and devastating hooks. Bowe was also known for his ability to fight on the inside, using his size and strength to overpower his opponents. He was a skilled counterpuncher and had a good sense of timing, often catching his opponents off guard with quick and powerful punches.

Bowe's biggest issues were his lack of discipline out of the ring, including missing training and not dieting like a champion, which resulted in inconsistent performances.

Riddick Bowe was one of the more difficult fighters to rank and assess in this book. At his best you have to put him as the favourite over the majority of fighters, with very few exceptions. However, his best was short lived and outside Holyfield he lacked any other all-time great (or even solid) names.

Rocky Marciano

Tale of the Tape

Prime age: 28

Fights: 49

Wins: 49

KOs: 43

Losses: 0

Draws: 0

KO percentage: 88%

Rounds boxed: 241

Height: 5 feet 10 inches

Weight: 184 pounds

Reach: 67 inches

Stance: Orthodox

Achievements

- World heavyweight champion.
- Only heavyweight in history to retire undefeated.
- Holds the record for highest KO-to-win ratio in world title fights, at eighty-five percent.

Statistics

Power: 95

Speed: 75

Chin: 100

Heart: 100

Stamina: 100

Ring IQ: 75

Total: 545/600 = 91%

Known as the "Brockton Blockbuster" or "the Rock", Rocky Marciano was a great tough fighter. While not the fastest or most skilful, he was as tough as they come with an iron chin and unlimited stamina and heart. The only heavyweight in history to retire undefeated, Marciano should be in everyone's top ten heavyweights list.

During forty-nine fights, Rocky was down only twice – and both times got off the canvas to KO his opponent. In their exhibition match, Ali commented on how hard Marciano hit, considering he was long retired and in his mid-forties at the time.

A prime Marciano would be a handful for just about anyone. A mix of relentless pressure and body punching combined with a destructive right cross meant Rocky could give anyone a torrid night in the ring.

Great wins over Jersey Joe Walcott (twice), Ezzard Charles (twice), Archie Moore and Joe Louis demonstrate his greatness.

However, it can be argued that all his best wins were against past-their-prime heavyweights, and two of them were able to knock him down (Walcott and Charles, respectively). Also, you have to take into consideration that his biggest win in Joe Louis occurred at a point when Louis was far out of his prime and really shouldn't have been boxing. That said, you can only beat the opponents in front of you, and retiring undefeated is no easy feat.

An obvious weakness that could be exploited is his lack of size. At the time this wasn't too much of an issue, with fighters being smaller than the super heavyweights of today. At five feet ten and 184 pounds, Marciano would now be considered a small cruiserweight.

Combining this with slow feet, short arms, a lack of technical skills and a tendency to get hit clean would really work against him when compared with other all-time great heavyweights.

Rocky was also vulnerable to getting cut quite easily, but as a wolverine in the ring, he would never take a backwards step. As a result, he is a fantastic addition to this list.

Sonny Liston

Tale of the Tape

Prime age: 32

Fights: 54

Wins: 50

KOs: 39

Losses: 4

Draws: 0

KO percentage: 72%

Rounds boxed: 265

Height: 6 feet 1 inch

Weight: 214 pounds

Reach: 84 inches

Stance: Orthodox

Achievements

- World heavyweight champion.
- Inaugural WBC heavyweight champion.

Statistics

Power: 95

Speed: 75

Chin: 95

Heart: 80

Stamina: 80

Ring IQ: 80

Total: 505/600 = 84%

Our next great fighter is the Big Bear, Sonny Liston. Born Charles L. Liston in 1930 (exact birthdate is unknown) in Sand Slough, Arkansas, Liston had a troubled childhood, growing up in poverty and facing numerous challenges. He turned to boxing as a way to escape his difficult circumstances and make a better life for himself.

Liston's professional boxing career began in 1953, and he quickly gained attention for his impressive punching power and intimidating presence in the ring. Standing at six feet one inch tall and weighing around 215 pounds, Liston was known for his incredible strength and knockout ability. He had a reach of 84 inches, which gave him a significant advantage over his opponents.

He was known for his aggressive and powerful fighting style, relying on his immense strength and punching power to overwhelm foes. Liston had a reputation for being a fearsome and intimidating fighter with a ramrod jab and devastating right hand, which he used to deliver knockout blows. Liston was also known for his defensive skills, utilising a high guard and quick reflexes to avoid punches.

Liston was particularly effective at fighting on the inside, where he could use his size and strength to his advantage. He would often work his way inside his opponent's guard and unleash a barrage of powerful punches, aiming to overwhelm with sheer force.

He was also skilled at cutting off the ring, effectively trapping his opponents in corners or against the ropes, where he could unleash his powerful shots with maximum impact. His relentless pressure and ability to close the distance quickly made him a formidable opponent in close-quarters combat.

During his rise to the top, the champ understandably refused to fight him, so Liston did the next best thing: he literally ran through the whole division, taking out top rated contenders such as Cleveland Williams (twice), Nino Valdes, Willi Besmanoff, Howard King (twice), Roy Harris, Zora Folley, Eddie Machen and finally Albert Westphal, all within the space of two and half years, averaging a fight every three months.

When Floyd Patterson finally relented and granted him a title shot, he was destroyed in one round and again in the rematch.

Unfortunately for Liston, after easily becoming the best fighter in the world, a young Cassius Clay arrived on the scene and dethroned him when Sonny refused to come out for the seventh round during their bout.

A rematch with Clay (by now known as Muhammed Ali) resulted in the controversial phantom punch.

This was followed by a string of wins against sub-par opponents, with a surprising loss to Leotis Martin. A final win over Chuck Wepner rounds out a meteoric rise to the top and equally dramatic fall.

Liston's career came to a tragic end when he was found dead in his Las Vegas home in January 1971. However, his impact on the sport of boxing, particularly during his reign as heavyweight champion, cannot be overlooked. Sonny Liston will always be remembered as one of the most powerful and feared boxers of his time.

Vitali Klitschko

Tale of the Tape

Prime age: 32

Fights: 47

Wins: 45

KOs: 41

Losses: 2

Draws: 0

KO percentage: 87%

Rounds boxed: 235

Height: 6 feet 7 inches

Weight: 248 pounds

Reach: 80 inches

Stance: Orthodox

Achievements

- World heavyweight champion.

Statistics

Power: 92

Speed: 75

Chin: 100

Heart: 95

Stamina: 85

Ring IQ: 85

Total: 535/600 = 89%

Next up is Vitali Klitschko. Born on the 19th of July 1971 in Belovodsk, Kyrgyzstan, Klitschko's early life was marked by athleticism, and he excelled in kickboxing before transitioning to boxing.

Klitschko's boxing career is nothing short of extraordinary. Standing at six feet seven inches tall, he possessed a remarkable combination of strength, agility and intelligence inside the ring. Vitali turned professional in 1996 after a successful amateur career.

Throughout his professional career, Klitschko faced some of the toughest opponents the heavyweight division had to offer. His remarkable record of forty-five wins, with forty-one of those victories coming by way of knockout, speaks volumes about his dominance in the ring.

Klitschko's fights were often characterised by powerful punches, a strategic approach and unwavering determination.

Klitschko's most memorable fight was his clash with Lennox Lewis in 2003, which ended due to a cut suffered by Klitschko. Being ahead on the scorecard and giving Lewis huge problems throughout the fight due to his size and reach, some argue Vitali would have beaten the great Lennox Lewis on that night had the fight continued.

Vitali's greatest strengths were his massive height and reach advantage, great power in both hands, a chin forged from cast iron, the heart of a lion and impressive stamina for someone his size.

His two biggest weaknesses were his slow hands and feet and lack of technical skills. This was not too much of an issue against most opponents, however against faster, more skilful and durable fighters, Vitali could come unstuck. Also, not having fought his toughest opponent during his era (his brother, understandably) does harm his legacy slightly.

Wladimir Klitschko

Tale of the Tape

Prime age: 35

Fights: 69

Wins: 64

KOs: 53

Losses: 5

Draws: 0

KO percentage: 77%

Rounds boxed: 370

Height: 6 feet 6 inches

Weight: 243 pounds

Reach: 81 inches

Stance: Orthodox

Achievements

- Two-time world heavyweight champion.
- Olympic gold medallist.
- Longest reigning cumulative heavyweight champion in history at 4382 days.
- Second most successful title defences, at twenty-three.

Statistics

Power: 92

Speed: 85

Chin: 70

Heart: 85

Stamina: 85

Ring IQ: 95

Total: 512/600 = 85%

Next up is Dr Steelhammer, Wladimir Klitschko. Klitschko had a very successful amateur career, winning the gold medal at the 1996 Olympics in Atlanta, Georgia. He turned professional later that year and quickly rose through the ranks, winning his first world title in 2000.

Wladimir was known for his powerful and precise jab, which he often used to set up his other punches. He also had a strong right hand, which he threw with great force and accuracy. Klitschko was a skilled counterpuncher and was able to quickly capitalise on opponent's mistakes. He was also known for his excellent footwork, which allowed him to move around the ring and avoid his opponent's punches.

Overall, Klitschko's fighting style was technical and strategic, relying on his precision and power to dominate his opponents.

Klitschko was also known for his defensive skills, often using his height and reach to keep his opponents at bay. He was a patient fighter, often waiting for his opponent to make a mistake before launching a counterattack.

Studying Wladimir's resume is a tale of two halves, the first before the late great Emanuel Steward and the second after he took over training responsibilities. Bringing on Steward was a masterstroke and gave Wladimir the confidence to adapt his fighting style to his own strengths, mainly his superior height, reach and boxing skills. A safety-first approach with a style known as "jab and grab" didn't always make for entertaining fights, however it was highly effective.

Key wins over other great fighters such as Kubrat Pulev, David Haye, Hasim Rahman, Lamon Brewster, Alexander Povetkin, Ruslan Chagaev and Chris Byrd round out a set of good-to-great wins, but no all-time great names. Having never fought the other all-time great heavyweight during his era (his brother, Vitali) is understandable, but does make you question how he would have handled another prime all-time great fighter.

Some noticeable unavenged losses to Lamon Brewster and Corrie Sanders at the start of his career also put a damper on his overall resume. This was bookended with two losses at the end of his career to Tyson Fury and Anthony Joshua, both great fighters in their own right. This completes a career that is historic, but also a bit underwhelming.

Ranking the Fighters Based on Career Achievements

U nlike the rest of the book, the aim of this section isn't to analyse if one fighter would have beaten another, but rather how their career and body of work compares to the other nineteen fighters. And let me start by saying this was no easy task. With so many great fighters, it is an almost impossible job to decide who actually achieved the most. Every time I look at the list I want to change the order.

A perfect example is that someone might consider Rocky Marciano's undefeated record as the greatest achievement, whereas it can be argued he was only undefeated because the division was relatively weak, and he never faced an in-prime all-time great fighter.

This left me with the question, is a win over a faded all-time great fighter better than a close loss to a prime all-time great fighter?

I have tried to be as unbiased and objective as possible, but if you have any suggestions, my email will be at the end of the book; please drop me a message.

So, without further ado, the fighter finishing in twentieth place is **Max Schmelling**. Schmelling was never the main man in the division, and his two best wins include Jack Sharkey (via DQ) and Joe Louis, however both fighters avenged their losses in the rematch. Schmelling was a great fighter, however his achievements are probably the least impressive overall when compared to the other fighters on this list.

Coming in at number nineteen is **Floyd Patterson**. Patterson was quite undersized and had a massive chin issue which severely hampered him. Had he avoided Sonny Liston he probably would be ranked higher on the list, however Patterson was a true warrior and didn't back down from any challenge. Unfortunately, impressive wins over Ingemar Johansson (twice) and Henry Cooper can't outweigh the devastating losses suffered to Liston, two one-sided defeats to Muhammad Ali and losses to Jerry Quarry and Jimmy Ellis. A perfectly respectable career, but not quite good enough to place higher on this list.

Our number eighteen combatant is **Ken Norton**. Similar to Patterson, it can be argued that he overachieved given his natural ability and chin vulnerabilities. Norton had great wins over Ali and Quarry, but also suffered two losses to Ali and was destroyed by George Foreman and Earnie Shavers. He did also put in a great performance in one of the greatest fights ever to a Prime Larry Holmes, which he lost.

Number seventeen is **Jim Jeffries**. For a fighter of his time to only have had twenty-four fights is quite surprising. But like they say, it's not about the quantity, but the quality – and Jeffries was the dominant fighter of his time. With great wins over James J. Corbett (twice), Bob Fitzsimmons (twice) and Tom Sharkey, he has a great record. His only loss was at the hands of Jack Johnson, six years after he initially retired.

Number sixteen is **Vitali Klitschko**. Klitschko's most famous fight was his loss to Lennox Lewis on cuts while being ahead on the judge's scorecards. A great fighter who, along with his brother, ruled a division during a down period with not many great fighters around. It is a real shame as they had the ability but not the opposition.

With the brothers not fighting each other, it is hard to rank either of them in the top ten. Klitschko's best wins include Shannon Briggs, Manuel Char and Derek Chisora, but two losses to Lennox Lewis and Chris Byrd round out not the greatest of resumes. However, twelve successful title defences and giving an all-time great like Lewis serious problems have to be taken into consideration in this ranking.

Our next fighter coming in at fifteenth place is **Jack Dempsey**. Dempsey was a great aggressive fighter who held nothing back. He was clearly the best fighter in the division when he was champ and enjoyed a nearly seven-year title reign, however that did include a three-year gap where he was effectively retired. With two losses to Gene Tunney and his best wins being Jess Willard and Jack Sharkey, it does make it difficult to justify placing Dempsey any higher on the list.

Numbers fourteen to five were tricky to rank, with a legitimate case for any of these fighters being placed higher or lower.

Number fourteen is Big Daddy **Riddick Bowe**. In terms of head to head, I would place Bowe higher, however his career didn't have the impact that his ability and potential suggested it might. Two big wins over a prime Evander Holyfield and a strong win over Herbie Hide complete a pretty wafer-thin resume. However, his only loss being to Holyfield, becoming the first boxer to win all four sanctioning belts at heavyweight (WBA, WBO, WBC and IBF) as well as an Olympic Silver medal do count in his favour.

Thirteenth place is Smokin' **Joe Frazier**. If we were ranking this list on heart alone, Frazier would undoubtedly be number one, however this isn't the case. Even though he was clearly the best in the division for a short amount of time, this coincided with Muhammad Ali's ban. He also suffered two losses to Ali and two devastating KO losses to George Foreman. Number thirteen seems a fair placing considering his achievements as world champion, Olympic gold medallist and his win over Ali in the *Fight of the Century* – in my opinion the single greatest win in heavyweight history.

Coming in at number twelve is **Wladimir Klitschko**. This is an interesting one. He had some outstanding achievements, like being a two-time world champion, Olympic gold medallist, the longest reigning cumulative champion in history at 4383 days and having the second most successful title defences at twenty-three. Normally such achievements would warrant a higher placing, but we have to look a little closer. Klitschko didn't beat one all-time great fighter, with his best wins being against Alexander Povetkin, David Haye and Kubrat Pulev. He also didn't avenge any of his defeats aside from the one against Lamon Brewster. I guess it comes down to what you think ranks higher: pure stats or real opposition faced.

Just missing out of the top ten is **Sonny Liston**. A great and intimidating warrior who wasn't afraid of taking on anyone, Liston was a formidable fighter and truly an all-time great. Floyd Patterson's management team wanted nothing to do with Liston and avoided him for as long as possible, so what did Sonny do? He ran through the rest of the division with ease, forcing the title shot. Two great wins over Patterson, as well as Chuck Wepner and Cleveland Williams (twice) round out a respectable resume. Sonny would probably be in the top ten, if not top five, if a certain Cassius Clay hadn't come along and upset the odds.

Number ten is the defensive master, **Jack Johnson**. Johnson was the first ever Black world heavyweight champion, reigning for seven years. He holds great wins over Sam Langford, Bob Fitzsimmons and James J. Jeffries, all the while suffering from extreme racism. Johnson only actually had ten fights during his seven-year reign and did have some losses and draws at the start of his career, which can be difficult to analyse. I think tenth is a fair placing, as on his night Johnson could give problems to any fighter in the history of the sport.

Potentially a controversial one, my number nine pick is Iron **Mike Tyson**. Tyson would probably refuse to place himself, given how humble and respectful to other great fighters he is. Luckily, I'm happy to do it for him. Tyson burst onto the scene and quickly established himself as the man in the division. His achievements speak for themselves: youngest world heavyweight champion in history; first heavyweight boxer to hold WBA, WBC and IBF titles, unifying them in succession; and being a two-time heavyweight champ.

However, even though he racked up some great wins, none were truly all-time great boxers, aside from Larry Holmes, who was past his prime and took the fight on short notice. His two toughest opponents in Evander Holyfield and Lennox Lewis both knocked him out. It is a real shame we never got to see Tyson at his best for longer, but what we got was exciting, destructive and one of a kind.

Entering at number eight is **Gene Tunney**. Tunney's achievements speak for themselves: world heavyweight champion, undefeated as a heavyweight and only one loss in eighty-eight fights (to Harry

Greb, who he subsequently beat twice). Tunney had a brilliant career with two great wins over Jack Dempsey and Harry Greb. He was one of the few heavyweight champs to retire on top, alongside Rocky Marciano and Lennox Lewis. This firmly places him in the top ten.

Smashing his way to number seven is **Rocky Marciano**. The Rock is the only heavyweight champion in history to retire undefeated, at forty-nine wins – an incredible achievement, especially when you consider he didn't duck anyone. With the highest KO percentage in world title fights at eighty-five percent, he would be a tough night's work for anyone. With great wins over Jersey Joe Walcott (twice), Ezzard Charles (twice), Archie Moore and Joe Louis, the only things stopping me placing Rocky higher is that his main wins came against fighters towards the end of their careers, and that he was on top when the division was pretty weak. If Marciano was to face Louis at his best, I believe Louis would have won a tough fight.

Jabbing his way to number six is **Larry Holmes**. Holmes' biggest issue was that he came after Muhammad Ali and before Mike Tyson, two of the most charismatic and exciting champions in history. This is a real shame as he was a formidable fighter with some remarkable achievements such as his seven-year reign as champ, when he was clearly the best in the division. He also handed Ali his only stoppage loss, albeit against a completely shot Ali who had no business being in the ring that night. Additionally, he had a streak of forty-eight fights undefeated, which should have been forty-nine if it wasn't for his disrespectful remarks about Marciano. Great wins over Ken Norton, Earnie Shavers (twice), Ali, Trevor Berbick, Leon Spinks and Gerry Cooney go alongside losses to Spinks (twice), Tyson and Holyfield.

Kicking off our top five is the Real Deal **Evander Holyfield**. Holyfield is the only four-time world heavyweight champion in history, the first fighter to win the undisputed championship in two weight classes (cruiserweight and heavyweight) and an Olympic silver medallist (which should have been gold). Holyfield boasts one the greatest resumes in the history of the heavyweight division, with wins over Buster Douglas, George Foreman, Riddick Bowe, Larry Holmes, Ray Mercer, Mike Tyson (twice); draws to Lennox Lewis, John Ruiz and Hasim Rahman; and losses to Bowe (twice), Michael Moorer, Lewis, Ruiz and James Toney. A true warrior with the heart of a lion and a simply incredible career.

Manoeuvring himself to number four is none other than **Lennox Lewis**. In most people's lists, Lewis would crack the top three, but I feel the other three boxers achieved slightly more. Lewis was a three-time world heavyweight champion, two-time lineal heavyweight champion undisputed heavyweight world champion and an Olympic gold medallist. His resume is absolutely brilliant, with wins over Evander Holyfield, Mike Tyson, Frank Bruno, Tony Tucker, Oliver McCall, Tommy Morrison, Shannon Briggs, David Tua, Hasim Rahman, Ray Mercer, Vitali Klitschko and Donovan Ruddock. His only two losses to McCall and Rahman were avenged in brutal fashion.

A couple of things holding Lewis back are that his two biggest wins, over Holyfield and Tyson, were when both fighters were clearly on the decline. He also never faced Bowe in the pro ranks, though not for want of trying. Additionally, the two shocking losses to decent but not world-level opponents do work against Lewis. Still, coming at four is a great achievement and Lewis could very well be the best heavyweight when ranking fighters on a head-to-head basis.

Smashing his way to third place is Big **George Foreman**. I went back and forth between Foreman and Lewis, however, all things considered, I felt George had the edge with a terrific set of achievements, the likes of which may never be eclipsed. Foreman was a two-time heavyweight world champion, the oldest person to hold the heavyweight title, an Olympic gold medallist and competed successfully in the division's two greatest eras: the seventies and nineties.

Foreman had a stellar resume, with big wins over Joe Frazier (twice), Ken Norton, Ron Lyle, Dwight Muhammad Qawi, Michael Moorer and Lou Savarese. Some losses to Muhammad Ali and Jimmy Young during his heyday and then after his comeback to Tommy Morrison and Shannon Briggs, combined with an impressive showing against a prime Evander Holyfield round out an unbelievable career that feels more like a Hollywood movie than real life.

Coming in at number two is the Brown Bomber **Joe Louis**. For some people Louis should be ranked first, and I can see their argument, however I personally feel second is the fairest placing. Louis had an extraordinary career, becoming heavyweight world champion, having a twelve-year reign as clearly the best fighter in the division and twenty-five successful title defences – a record which still stands to this day.

Louis only suffered three losses in his career: first, to Max Schmelling, who he came back to KO in one round, then to Ezzard Charles and Rocky Marciano, though both losses were suffered when Louis was clearly not the fighter he had been in his prime.

Big wins over Schmelling, Primo Carnera, Max Baer, Jack Sharkey and Jersey Joe Walcott (twice) solidify Louis as one of the absolute best heavyweights to ever lace up a pair of gloves.

I guess you have already figured out who number one is. Was there ever any doubt?

He was an Olympic gold medallist, after which he signed a record-breaking promotional deal to launch his pro career with massive fanfare.

He produced one of the most magnificent displays of boxing prowess ever witnessed with his awe-inspiring third round KO of Williams in a career-best performance.

Journalists and boxing aficionados were in wonder of the sublime skill on display.

He was brash, arrogant and not afraid to tell people how great he was.

My vote for the greatest heavyweight boxer of all time (in terms of achievements) is none other than...

Audley Harrison.

[Cue music screeching to a stop.]

(Sorry, I just had to do that!)

Obviously, number one is the greatest himself, **Muhammad Ali**.

Ali had a great list of achievements that put him firmly in the number one spot. He was the first ever three-time world heavyweight champion, first ever three-time lineal heavyweight champion, Olympic gold medallist and National Golden Gloves light heavyweight champion.

He fought and defeated more all-time great fighters than any other heavyweight and was clearly the best in his division during the seventies, known as the golden age for heavyweight boxing. Ali's wins are second to none and include George Foreman, Joe Frazier (twice), Sonny Liston (twice), Ken Norton (twice), Leon Spinks, Floyd Patterson (twice) and Earnie Shavers.

Ali suffered five losses, three of which he avenged (Frazier, Norton and Spinks), with the other two to Larry Holmes and Trevor Berbick, when Ali was well past his prime.

An interesting thing that is somewhat overlooked is the top ten *Ring Magazine* ranking from 1973 listed the following names: Foreman, Frazier, Norton, Jerry Quarry, Ron Lyle, Shavers, Oscar Bonavena, Joe Bugner, Jimmy Ellis and Chuck Wepner. Remarkably, Ali defeated every single one of these fighters, some more than once.

Looking at *Ring Magazine's* ranking from 1963, the names were Liston, Doug Jones, Ernie Terrell, Cleveland Williams, Zora Folley, Eddie Machen, Patterson, Karl Mildenberger, George Chuvalo and Brian London. Ali defeated all but Machen.

How truly incredible to clean out the division on two separate occasions, ten years apart. This has never been done before and probably never will be again.

Ali was a real warrior who wasn't afraid of fighting anyone. Going against two of the most feared fighters in history in Liston and Foreman and stopping both takes massive heart and courage, especially considering Ali was the heavy underdog in both fights. I personally don't think there will ever be a fighter as great as Ali, and he is absolutely the greatest heavyweight of all time.

Fantasy League

With the intros behind us we can now look towards the fun part. How would a head-to-head with all these great fighters have played out?

The next section of the book is set up as a league with each fighter fighting all nineteen opponents on this list and a ranking created. There will be nineteen separate fight cards, both with a co-main and main event. The league standings will be discussed after every five fights.

All fights feature an analysis of the match-up and a description of what I believe would have happened. For the most interesting fights and whenever it makes sense to do so, a more detailed simulation of the fight has been added, written in italics.

I have used AI to help predict how some fights would have gone, however the final decision was mine and on more than one occasion the AI result was overruled.

This is clearly speculation, and you can never know for certain how a fight would have played out. However, most times you can make an educated guess. A recent example is Joe Joyce vs. Zhieli Zhang II. My prediction was a win for Zhang, most likely by late stoppage, however for him to KO Joyce in three rounds was totally unpredictable.

I have considered each outcome carefully and never assumed that, for example, if Foreman beats Frazier and Norton, then by default he will easily defeat Ali.

If you disagree with a fight outcome, please understand there is literally no right or wrong answer, and this experiment is simply to recognise the greatness of all these fighters and to generate interest and debate.

Other things to note are:

- All fighters are in their prime and will have one fight with each opponent. If they have already fought in their primes (or close to) then the result of the real fight or the average of multiple fights will be considered.

- Styles make fights, and some fighters can deal with certain styles more effectively than others. This is taken into account when deciding outcomes.

- Each fighter is aware of the strengths and weaknesses of their opponent and is assumed to have had a full twelve-week training camp.

- Fights are contested over twelve rounds with no three-knockdown rule.

- A win is three points and a loss is zero points.

- If two fighters end on the same points, then the winner of their fight will finish ahead in the league standings.

- If three fighters have the same score, then the placing will be based on whoever beat the tougher opposition. This will be measured by their opponent's records.

With that said...

Ladies and gentleman, it's fighting time.

FIGHT CARD ONE

Evander Holyfield vs. Joe Frazier

Jim Jeffries vs. Joe Louis

Max Schmeling vs. Ken Norton

Lennox Lewis vs. Floyd Patterson

George Foreman vs. Jack Johnson

Vitali Klitschko vs. Gene Tunney

Jack Dempsey vs. Larry Holmes

Wladimir Klitschko vs. Muhammad Ali

Co-main Event: Rocky Marciano vs. Sonny Liston

Main Event: Mike Tyson vs. Riddick Bowe

Evander Holyfield vs. Joe Frazier

What a fight to kick things off! A genuine fifty/fifty contest that could go either way. Both fighters have shown tremendous heart and willingness to engage in a war more than almost any other two boxers.

Holyfield is bigger and has a longer reach, as well as better skills. He will use his head to stun and push back Frazier like he did against Tyson. However, Frazier won't be phased by Holyfield's power and will turn the fight into an all-out brawl, something that Holyfield can never resist.

Physically both are on the smaller side, with Frazier standing at five feet eleven and 205 pounds, compared to Holyfield at six feet two-and-a-half inches and 217 pounds. Holyfield also has the longer reach by four inches.

Smokin' Joe starts the fight slow and is on the end of Holyfield's jab for the first few rounds. Holyfield follows up his jab with quick hooks that bounce off Frazier's chin.

From Round Four onwards, Frazier fully settles into the fight and is really working over the body with some debilitating shots. His left hook is like a homing missile that he continuously lands, much to Holyfield's annoyance.

As the fight enters the latter rounds, Holyfield is starting to slow – an effect of the relentless body attacks. His corner urge him to stay off the ropes and keep the fight at mid to long range, imploring him to use his jab.

But being the warrior that he is, this just doesn't compute. He wants to take out Frazier and isn't willing to take a backwards step or box his way to a win. His only goal is to out gun his smaller foe. The Real Deal rallies late in the fight, putting together some excellent combinations as well as the odd subtle clash of heads.

Frazier doesn't care; he feels he has his man exactly where he wants him and ramps up the pressure: left hook to the body, right hook to the body and BAM! A hard left hook to the head that snaps Holyfield's head back.

Holyfield stands firm and fires off a left-right. Both land and the crowd is on their feet, cheering both pugilists.

As the fight reaches its climax, neither fighter lets up. Both stand centre of the ring and trade shot for shot, punch for punch. As the bell rings they collapse into each other's arms and show the respect they have for the other.

A really tough fight to call that could go either way. Both had their moments, but Frazier landed the more eye-catching shots and clearly hurt Holyfield on more than one occasion.

Verdict: Split decision win to Frazier.

Jim Jeffries vs. Joe Louis

Jeffries is tailor-made for Louis, being slower and with less technical skills. The only area I would give him the slight advantage is stamina and chin, but even then, it's marginal. Louis will easily piece Jeffries up with fast combinations and hard, clean shots. It will almost be target practice for Louis.

Verdict: TKO win to Louis in Round Five.

Max Schmeling vs. Ken Norton

A closer fight than you would initially think, with both fighters being fairly evenly matched. Neither are known for their technical skills and both have lost most of their big fights. Norton's size, stamina and awkward style will see him through a messy and scrappy fight.

Verdict: Decision win to Norton.

Lennox Lewis vs. Floyd Patterson

An easy fight to predict. Patterson's only advantage is speed, but he is totally undersized and has a very weak chin. Going up against a devastating puncher like Lewis will only end in one way: with a brutal KO.

Verdict: KO win to Lewis in Round Two.

George Foreman vs. Jack Johnson

This is an interesting fight. Johnson is very defensive and technical, and his game plan will be to take Foreman into the latter rounds and tire him out, similar to how Ali defeated him. The problem being that Johnson won't have enough power to worry Foreman, and his durability or chin is nowhere near as good as Ali's.

I can see Johnson frustrating Foreman for two to three rounds before Big George sledgehammers his way through his defence and stops him.

Verdict: TKO win to Foreman in Round Five.

Vitali Klitschko vs. Gene Tunney

This is a tough matchup for Tunney. He holds the technical skills, ring IQ, stamina and speed over the slower Klitschko, however Dr Ironfist is simply too big, with seven inches of height and fifty pounds of weight over Tunney (mostly muscle).

Tunney might circle and avoid Klitschko for a few rounds, but eventually he will get caught and there's no way he can stand up to someone with an eighty-seven percent KO ratio.

Verdict: KO win to V. Klitschko in Round Five.

Jack Dempsey vs. Larry Holmes

An interesting fight with a definite clash of styles: the aggressive brawler in Dempsey against the silky-smooth boxing skills of Holmes.

I see this fight going a similar way to the Dempsey-Tunney fight. Holmes' great jab and fast hands and feet will easily keep the Manassa Mauler at bay. However, Holmes' biggest weakness is his lack of KO power, so I can see Dempsey having his moments in the fight and maybe even getting a knockdown.

Verdict: Unanimous decision win to Holmes.

Wladimir Klitschko vs. Muhammad Ali

This will be a great fight, not for the action, but to see Ali against a bigger boxer who possesses great technical skills and a powerful right hand.

Klitschko would be a tough night's work for pretty much any fighter and would be favourite against most. However, with Ali he's against a fighter that is easily faster than him and has a better chin, stamina, heart and ring IQ.

Ali takes maybe three or four rounds to adjust to Dr Steelhammer's jab-and-grab style. With his fast feet he simply keeps circling around his bigger and slower opponent, striking with lightning-fast combinations.

It is a tough fight, with Ali having to eat a few big shots, however his speed and ability to adjust to his opponents see him through.

Verdict: Unanimous decision win to Ali.

Co-main Event: Rocky Marciano vs. Sonny Liston

What a great fight! This could easily have been the main event. It is a real shame this fight didn't happen in real life, as they missed each other by a few years.

Liston holds the size advantage, but Marciano has the slight power advantage and easily has superior stamina, heart, work rate and chin.

This is a scenario where perhaps the most intimidating heavyweight (Liston) goes up against a guy who has no fear and won't back down from anyone (Marciano). A case of irresistible force meets immovable object.

The fight starts in Marciano's favour, with him banking some early rounds with his work rate. Marciano attacks Liston's body and attempts to slow him down while also looking for his overhand right.

However, Liston possesses a great jab and uppercuts and, with the help of his massive eighty-four inch reach, starts landing on Marciano's chin at will.

Marciano is too slow and easy to hit. In two of his toughest fights he suffered a knockdown, and Liston drops him more than once. The fight is called off in the latter rounds after a gallant display.

Verdict: TKO win to Liston in Round Nine.

Main Event: Mike Tyson vs. Riddick Bowe

Our first main event is an absolute classic, with two of the greatest heavyweights putting it all on the line.

Fun fact: both hail from the same area of Brooklyn. Given they were both active in the nineties, it is a true shame we never got to witness this fight. An argument can be made for either fighter coming out on top, and I wouldn't disagree.

In one corner you have Iron Mike Tyson, a literal buzzsaw of a fighter; fast, powerful, with great head movement and amazing combination punching. He's against Bowe, a bigger, stronger opponent with unrivalled inside fighting, great heart, a strong chin and just as good power.

A real fifty/fifty fight that could go either way. In a fight like this, there will be no losers.

So how would such a fight have played out?

One of Tyson's biggest strengths is his intimidation factor, with prior opponents beaten before the first bell. However, Bowe is not intimidated; if anything, this spurs him on.

Tyson starts fast, his hand speed and combination punching coming into play with great effect. But when Bowe ties up Tyson, this plays right into his biggest strengths, with inside fighting and uppercuts being Bowe's most dangerous weapons.

Bowe was knocked down against Holyfield, and at times you can definitely see Tyson scoring a knockdown, however with Bowe's great heart, he rides out the onslaught and takes over the mid rounds.

Tyson starts getting frustrated, however Bowe can't approach the fight like he did against Holyfield, mainly because Tyson hits too hard. A late knockdown for Tyson gets him over the line, barely.

Verdict: Split decision win to Tyson.

FIGHT CARD TWO

Larry Holmes vs. Muhammad Ali

Sonny Liston vs. Jim Jeffries

Joe Louis vs. Max Schmeling

Ken Norton vs. George Foreman

Floyd Patterson vs. Vitali Klitschko

Jack Johnson vs. Mike Tyson

Gene Tunney vs. Jack Dempsey

Joe Frazier vs. Lennox Lewis

Co-main Event: Riddick Bowe vs. Wladimir Klitschko

Main Event: Rocky Marciano vs. Evander Holyfield

Larry Holmes vs. Muhammad Ali

What a fight this would have been! Prime for prime a real pick 'em.

Even though both combatants did fight in 1980, anyone who has seen the fight knows it should never have been allowed to happen. Ali was clearly past his prime and was showing early signs of Parkinson's. It was one of the saddest fights to occur in the history of this great sport, and is a shame it happened.

Luckily, we are comparing both fighters in their respective primes, and Ali's was in 1966–77, before his ban from boxing. So, how will this go down?

Ali knows how tough an opponent Holmes is and will not take him lightly. Holmes possesses perhaps the greatest jab in heavyweight history, and when combining this with good fundamentals, fast hands and feet and a great heart, you have a well-rounded fighter.

Compared to Ali, Holmes is more skilful with a longer reach. They are both the same height and weight, and they are about even in terms of power. However Ali is clearly ahead in terms of speed, reflexes and chin.

The fight goes the distance, with Holmes successfully controlling the tempo with his solid jab and boxing skills.

However, once Ali makes some adjustments, his super-fast combinations and footwork make him a hard target to land on. Ali also strikes with some precise and stinging shots, puffing up the Easton Assassin's face.

With Holmes' lack of power, Ali isn't too phased about getting hit and is more than happy to take a shot to land two of his own.

Verdict: Unanimous decision win to Ali.

Sonny Liston vs. Jim Jeffries

This will be a closer fight than expected. Both fighters are the same height and a similar weight (with Jeffries being ten pounds heavier), though Liston holds the reach advantage.

Jeffries will have no fear of entering the ring against the Big Bear and will push Liston into the latter rounds with the help of his strong chin and great stamina.

Where Liston prevails is with his powerful jabs and uppercuts, and he will slowly wear Jeffries down. Jeffries also has slow hand and foot speed as well as a lack of boxing skills, so won't be able to keep Liston off him once hurt.

Verdict: TKO win to Liston in Round Ten.

Joe Louis vs. Max Schmeling

This is an interesting one. Both fighters fought each other twice in their primes and each hold a win over the other.

Schmeling won the first fight with a great performance, exploiting Louis' weakness of bringing his left jab to his waist after throwing it, leaving himself open to the counter overhand right. Schmeling brutally took advantage of this flaw and battered Louis for twelve rounds.

The rematch was very different, with Louis earning a TKO in the first round.

The fairest thing would be to give both fighters a draw, however Louis was clearly the better fighter and the first fight happened when he was just twenty-four years old, so not quite the finished article he would become.

When looking at their careers and opponents defeated, Louis clearly has the edge, so with all things considered, had they known of each other's strengths and weaknesses and fought ten times, Louis would win more often than lose.

Verdict: TKO win to Louis in Round Six.

Ken Norton vs. George Foreman

The fight between them happened in both their primes.

Verdict: TKO win to Foreman in Round Two.

Floyd Patterson vs. Vitali Klitschko

This fight will play out similar to the Lewis fight. Patterson has speed and boxing skills over Klitschko, however the massive size difference, Klitschko's iron chin and thumping power will make light work of Patterson.

Verdict: KO win to V. Klitschko in Round One.

Jack Johnson vs. Mike Tyson

An interesting fight, since the two are similar sized, with Johnson being slightly taller but Tyson heavier by about ten pounds. The reach is in Johnson's favour by three inches.

Johnson starts the fight by controlling the pace and using his great defensive skills and ring IQ to keep Tyson at bay. The main problem the Galveston Giant has is he doesn't hit hard enough to worry Tyson and is noticeably slower with not the strongest chin.

Iron Mike would work his way into a position to land a devastating KO.

Verdict: KO win to Tyson in Round Five.

Gene Tunney vs. Jack Dempsey

This fight happened twice, both times with the same result. However, Dempsey wasn't in his prime, being effectively retired for three years before fighting Tunney and even getting a nose job in that time. However, even if they fought when Dempsey was more active, the result most likely would have been the same.

Verdict: Unanimous decision win to Tunney.

Joe Frazier vs. Lennox Lewis

Frazier is a special talent and an incredible fighter who possesses the heart of a lion and has no fear of any man. However, Frazier's crouching come-forward aggressive style will fall right into the hands of Lewis, and winning will be a tall order for Smokin' Joe.

Lewis struggles most with tall boxers who have a strong right hand and stiff jab. Frazier will be giving up six inches in height, forty pounds in weight and ten inches in reach, and can't rely on his left hook or come-forward pressure style.

Lewis will simply keep the fight at a distance and when Frazier gets close will just tie him up, lean on him and tire him out. A fairly routine win for Lewis, who may need to eat a couple of left hooks and some body shots.

Verdict: KO win to Lewis in Round Three.

Co-main Event Riddick Bowe vs. Wladimir Klitschko

This will be another fifty/fifty fight that could go either way. Both fighters are exactly the same height, have the same reach and a similar weight. A real super heavyweight showdown with both fighters being big and skilful and possessing knockout power.

Breaking the fight down, Klitschko's biggest weapons are his sledgehammer right hand, great jab, hand speed and solid fundamentals. Bowe's strengths lie with his in-fighting, great heart, jab and strong uppercuts.

On balance, Bowe does possess two wins that are better than any of Klitschko's over a prime Evander Holyfield. Klitschko does also have a suspect chin, having suffered knockout losses to opponents that hit far lighter than Bowe.

Klitschko establishes his strong jab in the early rounds, frustrating Bowe with his jab-and-grab style and knocking Bowe down in the first half.

However, in the later rounds, Bowe finds success and starts taking the fight, working over Klitschko with his stronger inside fighting. Bowe comes on strong in round twelve and forces a stoppage, similar to how Anthony Joshua did.

Verdict: TKO win to Bowe in Round Twelve.

Main Event: Rocky Marciano vs. Evander Holyfield

This fight is totally deserving of the main event status on this fight card. The heart displayed between both of these great fighters in their careers was unreal. Neither will back down.

You have a true clash of styles, with the relentless brawler in Marciano bulldozing forward and throwing powerful punches to the body and overhand right crosses to the chin. Holyfield will keep the fight at a distance, use his longer reach, size and superior boxing skills to nullify the attacks and control the pace while also landing with his own combinations and sharp counters.

Holyfield has some clear advantages, with size, reach, boxing skills and speed ready to be deployed with great effect. The two biggest issues he has are his lack of knockout power and the fact that he can't help but get drawn into a war unnecessarily.

This fight will definitely make it to the latter stages and be absolutely epic.

Holyfield will use his boxing skills for the first few rounds to keep Marciano at bay, however Marciano will start to wear down

Holyfield, who slows down when attacked to the body – as seen in the Cooper, Toney and Bowe fights.

Holyfield also can't avoid being drawn into a slugfest, which is great for the fans but not the best idea when you are trading blows with someone who has an eighty-eight percent knockout percentage – the highest of any fighter on this list.

The Rock will start to take over the latter rounds, and with his superior stamina, chin and power, will grind Holyfield down in one of the greatest fights ever.

Verdict: TKO win to Marciano in Round Eleven.

FIGHT CARD THREE

Evander Holyfield vs. Sonny Liston

Max Schmeling vs. Jim Jeffries

Lennox Lewis vs. Rocky Marciano

Vitali Klitschko vs. Joe Frazier

Mike Tyson vs. Ken Norton

Jack Dempsey vs. Floyd Patterson

Wladimir Klitschko vs. Jack Johnson

Muhammad Ali vs. Gene Tunney

Co-main Event: Larry Holmes vs. Riddick Bowe

Main Event: George Foreman vs. Joe Louis

Evander Holyfield vs. Sonny Liston

What a fight to kick off Fight Card Three! Holyfield has been in one war after another; a bit unlucky to consecutively come up against three stylistic nightmare match-ups.

So, breaking down the tale of the tape, both fighters are fairly evenly sized; Holyfield has about an inch and a half in height and few pounds in weight over Liston, however the difference is negligible. The main difference is Liston's massive reach at eighty-four inches and huge fists measured at fifteen inches when closed – the largest of any heavyweight champion.

Liston's biggest strength is his intimidation factor, but Holyfield will not be intimidated in the slightest. Stepping in the ring with a prime Bowe and Lewis, a still-great Tyson, a formidable Foreman and the tallest heavyweight champ in history in Valuev clearly showed balls the size of grapefruits. Liston might be unnerved himself at not being able to bully or intimidate his foe.

One thing is for sure, this has all-out war written all over it.

So how does the fight play out?

Holyfield sticks to his boxing, clearly able to outbox Liston without too many problems. Keeping the fight at a distance and using his superior boxing IQ, Holyfield controls the pace and frustrates the Big Bear.

However, Holyfield isn't able resist entering into a firefight with Liston, and this is where the fight gets interesting. Liston is clearly the stronger and harder puncher and has Holyfield backing up. He scores a knockdown or two during the fight.

The fight is definitely not finishing early. Towards the championship rounds, Holyfield starts to take over and outlands Liston, forcing the stoppage.

Verdict: TKO win to Holyfield in Round Twelve.

Max Schmeling vs. Jim Jeffries

An evenly-matched contest. Both have similar strengths and weaknesses and are comparable in size.

Jeffries brings great durability and stamina that will result in this being a tough fight. The difference will be Schmeling's boxing skills and ring IQ; Schmeling will use his superior skills to control the pace and land on Jeffries' chin with those big overhand rights.

Jeffries has his moments, but not enough to get the win.

Verdict: Decision win to Schmeling.

Lennox Lewis vs. Rocky Marciano

This fight is a bad stylistic fight for Marciano. His brawler style won't work against a bigger, stronger and more skilled super heavyweight. Lewis will just time Marciano and land with his polarising right hand flush on his chin.

Verdict: KO win to Lewis in Round Four.

Vitali Klitschko vs. Joe Frazier

Frazier's come-forward style will be his undoing here. Klitschko isn't the fastest or most technical of boxers, however he is massive at six feet seven inches and 248 pounds. There is no way Frazier could hurt Klitschko, especially considering his opponent's iron chin, and he is too small to be effective.

Verdict: KO win to V. Klitschko in Round Three.

Mike Tyson vs. Ken Norton

This card has been pretty easy to predict so far. Norton's weakness is powerful punchers, and Tyson can hit with maximum force with both fists.

Norton's awkward style and height as well as his longer reach might be a little difficult for Iron Mike to get around for a round or two, however his devastating combination punching, superior speed and defensive skills will be too much for the Black Hercules, who has chin issues when hit flush by big hitters.

Verdict: TKO win to Tyson in Round Four.

Jack Dempsey vs. Floyd Patterson

This will be a real clash of styles. You have the fast hands and skills of Patterson against the rugged aggression of Dempsey.

Both fighters are similar in size (Dempsey is two inches taller), both weigh the same and Dempsey has slightly longer reach, however not significantly enough to affect the outcome of the fight.

It is quite clear the approach each would take. Patterson will use his fast hands and skills to control the pace, stay on the outside and use movement to avoid Dempsey's attacks. Dempsey will pursue Patterson around the ring and miss more than land, however he will catch Patterson from time to time. The key is whether the Manassa Mauler will be able to finish off Patterson.

The fight will be similar to the Dempsey-Tunney fights.

The fight goes in Patterson's favour for most of the rounds. Dempsey's lack of technical skills as well as Patterson's faster hands and feet give Dempsey even more problems than he faced against Tunney.

As the fight enters the championship rounds, Patterson is breathing heavier than he would like; the constant movement and tying up his stronger foe has taken a real toll.

In Round Ten, Patterson mistakenly stays in the pocket for too long and after nine frustrating rounds, Dempsey finally sees his opening. The sniff of blood to the great white shark is irresistible. Dempsey scores the knockdown he's been chasing, and the tables have turned.

Patterson gamely makes it to his feet but is shaken up. In a daze, he backs off, throwing out his jab. But with nothing behind it, the Manassa Mauler lives up to his billing, cutting into position and landing a crushing left hook.

Patterson's mouth guard flies into the second row and before the ref can step in, another right from Dempsey sends Patterson crashing to the mat. The ref takes one look at Patterson's limp body and waves off the fight.

Verdict: KO win to Dempsey in Round Ten.

Wladimir Klitschko vs. Jack Johnson

Klitschko will come into this fight supremely confident. Johnson has never faced someone as big, powerful or skilled and Dr Steelhammer will land flush on Johnson's chin, sending him to the canvas for good.

Verdict: KO win to W. Klitschko in Round Four.

Muhammad Ali vs. Gene Tunney

Ali will have no issues dealing with Tunney. Tunney is a great skilled fighter, however he has never faced someone as big, fast or strong. Tunney's lack of power will give Ali literally nothing to worry about; he will just land combinations and do a number on the Fighting Marine.

Verdict: TKO win to Ali in Round Eight.

Co-main Event: Larry Holmes vs. Riddick Bowe

Two legends squaring off with distinct advantages and weaknesses over each other. It is a shame this fight never happened. Even when

Holmes was still around in the nineties, he could have given a decent account of himself.

In terms of size, at six feet five inches Bowe has two inches on Holmes, and is about twenty pounds heavier. However Holmes is the more skilled boxer with one of the best jabs in the division's history, slightly faster hands and feet and a much better resume, having shared the ring with the likes of Ali, Tyson and Holyfield.

Holmes also has vastly more experience in the pro ranks, with seventy-five fights and 579 rounds boxed compared to Bowe's forty-five fights and 195 rounds.

One thing working against Holmes is his average power, with only a fifty-nine percent KO ratio compared to Bowe's seventy-three percent.

In a fight as tight as this, you have to look at all the details. It is a difficult one to call and could go either way.

Bowe bulldozes forward, using his size to boss the fight. However Holmes is no mug and sees this coming. Using his speed and skills, he keeps Bowe at bay and avoids his powerful shots. Holmes knows that Bowe had issues with technical fighters like Galota and Holyfield, and he is just as skilled as them, if not more so.

Big Daddy has the Easton Assassin hurt on more than one occasion, and when they get up close Bowe easily outworks Holmes on the inside, landing some painful uppercuts that have Holmes reeling.

Unlike Holyfield, Holmes won't be dragged into a war and sticks to the game plan, outlanding Bowe mainly because of his excellent jab and faster hands.

Down the stretch, Holmes is ahead on the cards and Bowe really has to push the pace in search of a knockout. The only person to KO Holmes was Tyson, and this was an undertrained and past-his-prime Holmes. Bowe is not able to put away a prime Holmes.

Verdict: Decision win to Holmes.

Main Event: George Foreman vs. Joe Louis

This is a main event for the ages. A real dream fight, with both fighters known for their destructive power and ability to see off opponents in ruthless fashion.

Foreman has the size advantage with two inches in height, three inches in reach and about twenty pounds over Louis. However Louis has the better boxing skills, faster hands and combination punching, as well as better stamina.

The fight will come down to who can effectively execute their game plan long enough to see the other one off. Either way, this fight will be a barnstormer and a true cross-generation super fight.

Foreman comes barrelling forward using his size, strength and immense power to land his walking left hook/jab, stunning Louis early and scoring a first-round knockdown.

The Brown Bomber doesn't panic, having prepared for such a strategy and knowing he is in for a hard night's work. With his great powers of recovery, he sticks to his boxing and uses his sharp straight counters to exploit Foreman's wide looping shots, taking the fight into the second half, when Foreman's stamina comes into serious question.

Foreman has always had issues with movers, however Louis has slow feet, so he looks to tie up Foreman when up close and throw some fast combination punches on the break. Foreman is also wary of Louis' power and, during the middle rounds, Louis lands a huge right hand bomb, knocking Foreman down.

Big George gets up and fights on, but the damage is done, with Louis starting to take control of the fight and landing some stinging shots. With Foreman's stamina sapping away and Louis coming on strong, the ref finally waves it off after one tough, gruelling and classic fight.

Verdict: TKO win to Louis in Round Eight.

FIGHT CARD FOUR

Jack Johnson vs. Larry Holmes

Sonny Liston vs. Max Schmeling

Evander Holyfield vs. Lennox Lewis

Jim Jeffries vs. George Foreman

Gene Tunney vs. Riddick Bowe

Rocky Marciano vs. Vitali Klitschko

Ken Norton vs. Wladimir Klitschko

Floyd Patterson vs. Muhammad Ali

Co-main Event: Joe Frazier vs. Jack Dempsey

Main Event: Joe Louis vs. Mike Tyson

Jack Johnson vs. Larry Holmes

A very technical boxing fight to start Fight Card Four, with the defensive prowess of Johnson up against the silky boxing skills of Holmes.

Both fighters are similar sized, with Holmes having about two inches in height and a few pounds in weight advantage. Holmes also has a greater reach by seven inches, which could prove to be very telling. Neither fighter hits particularly hard and both have sturdy chins, so this won't be ending early.

The Easton Assassin establishes the pace early and uses his superior size and boxing skills to completely nullify Johnson's attacks. Johnson does excel in striking on the counter, however, and he uses his excellent defensive skills to be an elusive target.

Down the stretch, Johnson's fantastic conditioning comes into play, but him being behind on the scorecards puts on the pressure. With the Galveston Giant's lack of power, he isn't able to finish Holmes off, who hangs on to see the final bell.

Verdict: Decision win to Holmes.

Sonny Liston vs. Max Schmeling

The Max Schmeling who pummelled Joe Louis will be able to put up somewhat of a fight for a few rounds, however once Liston starts landing on Schmeling's chin with those power punches, this fight can only go one way.

Verdict: KO win to Liston in Round Five.

Evander Holyfield vs. Lennox Lewis

Now this would have been an interesting fight had Lewis fought the version of Holyfield that defeated Bowe.

The two fights they did have don't paint a true picture of how a fight between the two of them in their primes would have gone. Holyfield was already on the slide and clearly not his best by the time the two faced off in 1999, and this showed in his slower pace and less sharp shots. However in the second fight with Lewis, he did make it very competitive and some argue actually won the fight.

So will a younger Holyfield have enough in the tank to beat Lewis? Personally I think Lewis controlled both fights with his size, power and skills, and even a fresher Holyfield won't have enough to beat Lewis.

Verdict: Decision win to Lewis.

Jim Jeffries vs. George Foreman

Jeffries' lack of technical skills, hand and foot movement and power will give Foreman literally zero to worry about.

Verdict: KO win to Foreman in Round Two.

Gene Tunney vs. Riddick Bowe

Both are skilled fighters, with Tunney having the slight edge in speed, stamina and ring IQ. But Bowe towering over Tunney by five inches and weighing forty-five pounds more, as well as having more power, is hard to overlook.

Tunney will have to keep the fight at a distance and avoid Bowe's great in-fighting and uppercuts. This fight will look like two fighters from different weight divisions going against each other. The size and power will be too much for the Fighting Marine to overcome.

Verdict: TKO win to Bowe in Round Six.

Rocky Marciano vs. Vitali Klitschko

Neither fighter is known for their technical skills and both have devastating power and iron chins. It will be like Marciano fighting a much bigger version of himself.

Marciano and Klitschko have the two highest KO percentages in this book, so you can almost guarantee this fight isn't going the distance. Ultimately, Marciano will not be able to deal with the sixty pounds in weight, nine inches in height and seventeen inches in reach difference.

Verdict: KO win to V. Klitschko in Round Four.

Ken Norton vs. Wladimir Klitschko

This will be an interesting fight, as both have suspect chins and like to take their time in fights.

Norton's awkward style and amazing fitness levels will frustrate Klitschko, who won't want to take too many risks early on and will instead look to slowly break Norton down. Norton will have some early successes, however once Dr Steelhammer finds his range, he will start landing with that thudding overhand right and take out Norton.

Verdict: TKO win to W. Klitschko in Round Six.

Floyd Patterson vs. Muhammad Ali

This fight happened twice with the same result. Ali is too fast, strong and durable for Patterson, and the Rabbit doesn't have the firepower to inflict any damage on Ali.

Verdict: TKO win to Ali in Round Twelve.

Co-main Event: Joe Frazier vs. Jack Dempsey

A perfect tagline for this fight could be "ruthless aggression". Both fighters are all-action warriors with explosive left hooks. This fight will be *edge of your seat* stuff and a real nailbiter.

Looking at the tale of the tape, Dempsey has two inches in height, Frazier has about fourteen pounds in weight and their reach is the same. Dempsey is the harder hitter and a ruthless finisher, while

Frazier has more technical skills and slightly more heart and ring IQ. An evenly matched contest that could go either way.

So, what happens once the first bell rings?

Dempsey is a super-fast starter and with Frazier known to start slow, Dempsey sets a blistering pace, landing great power shots and knocking Smokin' Joe down a couple of times within the first three rounds.

Once Frazier has his legs back, he uses his weight advantage to push Dempsey back and work the body while also landing that killer left hook of his own. By Round Six, Frazier is firmly in control and knocks down Dempsey. However, the Manassa Mauler also possesses great stamina and heart and doesn't panic at Frazier coming on strong.

As the fight enters Round Eight, both are fighting on instinct and it turns into a firefight, with both landing bombs and the ref considering stopping the fight. The crowd is in a frenzy, both corners screaming at their fighters to slow things down and save some for the championship rounds. Neither listens, wanting to finish the other in one hell of a brutal back-and-forth war.

The deciding factor is Dempsey's power. Getting into a shoot-out with someone who hits harder and has sharper short shots is never a good idea, and this sees Dempsey home ... barely.

Verdict: TKO win to Dempsey in Round Nine.

Main Event: Joe Louis vs. Mike Tyson

Now we have a super main event between two fighters who truly transcend the sport of boxing. In the blue corner you have the Brown Bomber Joe Louis, considered by many as the greatest heavyweight of all time, with a twelve-year reign as champ and twenty-five defences. He's against Kid Dynamite Mike Tyson, the youngest ever heavyweight champ and the first fighter to unify all major belts.

This will be a true spectacle of a fight and one you can guarantee will not go the distance.

Studying the tale of the tape, Louis has four inches in height and five inches in reach over Tyson, however Tyson is about twenty pounds heavier and is built like a tank.

Both have great combination punching and extraordinary power, with seventy-five and seventy-six KO percentages, respectively. Tyson is slightly faster in hand speed and quite a bit faster with foot speed and also has a better chin, while Louis has more heart and stamina.

This will be an absolutely epic showdown, a real firefight with amazing boxing skills on display as well as concussive power. Like any fifty/fifty matchup, there will be testing times for both boxers, and by the end the real winners will be the fans.

Tyson comes out fast, throwing his brutal combinations and overwhelming Louis. He is a little overzealous, however, giving Louis the opportunity to land a couple of beautifully timed shots that knock Tyson down.

Straight away the crowd is on their feet, sensing an early finish. But Tyson is smart enough to clinch and clear his head, similar to in the first Bruno fight.

Once Tyson finds his legs, he uses his superior hand and foot speed to avoid Louis' powerful punches. Bobbing and weaving his way in and mixing up his body and head attacks, Tyson connects with some spectacular shots.

With Louis' poor head movement, Tyson lands a damaging left hook to the chin, knocking Louis down in the fourth round. Once Louis is back on his feet, he makes some adjustments and ties up Tyson on the inside with his longer reach, trying to frustrate him.

By Round Six both fighters are wary of the other's power, however Tyson still has enough in the tank to land some debilitating punches. Tyson's angles of attack give Louis, who always struggled with movers, some real problems.

Louis has never faced such a fast and ferocious fighter, and with Tyson's stronger chin absorbing Louis' combos, Kid Dynamite again drops Louis with a perfectly timed body shot, followed by a wicked uppercut. Louis gets up, however Iron Mike is a clinical finisher and forces the ref to step in, waving the fight off.

Verdict: TKO win to Tyson in Round Eight.

FIGHT CARD FIVE

Lennox Lewis vs. Sonny Liston

George Foreman vs. Max Schmeling

Vitali Klitschko vs. Evander Holyfield

Gene Tunney vs. Jack Johnson

Mike Tyson vs. Jim Jeffries

Wladimir Klitschko vs. Joe Louis

Larry Holmes vs. Ken Norton

Riddick Bowe vs. Floyd Patterson

Co-main Event: Muhammad Ali vs. Joe Frazier

Main Event: Jack Dempsey vs. Rocky Marciano

Lennox Lewis vs. Sonny Liston

A very tricky and interesting fight to kick off Fight Card Five. In one corner you have perhaps the most intimidating fighter in history in Sonny Liston going toe to toe with Lennox Lewis, a man who knows no fear and had to sue Mike Tyson to get him in the ring.

Both fighters are exceptionally strong and about even in terms of power, with each having a seventy-two KO percentage. Lewis is the better boxer with excellent ring IQ, as well as having height and weight on his side. But even though Liston is four inches shorter, they both have an eighty-four inch reach, which will cause Lewis some big problems.

Liston comes out fast and aims to get the fight stopped early. Once Lewis lands a big right hand in the first round, Liston becomes more wary of Lewis' power and stops charging in so recklessly.

Lewis already had the game plan set beforehand and avoids the Big Bear's most powerful shots, tying him up when close and employing some roughhouse tactics.

This fight isn't for the purists, but is very intriguing. With Liston's piston jab stopping Lewis in his tracks, the first three or four rounds are Liston's without too much trouble.

Lewis was out-jabbed by Bruno, Mercer and V. Klitschko, so isn't too worried at the start. Around the mid rounds the Lion makes some adjustments and uses his overhand right as well as his size and speed advantages to start catching Liston, really putting the pressure on him.

By Round Eight Liston is busted up pretty bad and refuses to come out to the bell, similar to during the first Ali fight.

Verdict: TKO win to Lewis in Round Nine.

George Foreman vs. Max Schmeling

Unfortunately for Schmeling, he holds no real advantages over Foreman. His superior stamina will not be enough to hold off a marauding Foreman, who will have no issue cutting off the ring and clubbing Schmeling into next week.

Verdict: KO win to Foreman in Three.

Vitali Klitschko vs. Evander Holyfield

Now this will be one hell of a fight. Both are true warriors who aren't afraid to mix it up with anyone.

Klitschko clearly possesses the height and weight advantage by about five inches and thirty pounds. Also in Klitschko's favour is an iron chin, some serious firepower in his fists (with an eighty-seven percent KO ratio), and the distinction of being the only fighter on this list to never be knocked down.

In Holyfield's defence, he is by far the more skilled boxer of the two. He's also faster, has better ring IQ and greater stamina.

The fight plays out similar to the Holyfield-Foreman contest, with Holyfield using his speed and skills to avoid Klitschko's power shots and using lateral movement to keep out of distance. When Klitschko steps in, the Real Deal lands three or four strong counters then moves out of position to reset.

As the fight wears on, Klitschko starts to tire and Holyfield piles on the pressure, landing some clean flashy shots for the judges.

Klitschko struggles to deal with the disparity in skills. His size isn't as effective given his slow foot and hand speed and lack of inside fighting. By the twelfth round, Klitschko is tired but is fighting on courageously. Unfortunately, he doesn't have enough to force the stoppage.

Verdict: Decision win to Holyfield.

Gene Tunney vs. Jack Johnson

This will be a technical fight with lots of feints, clinching and not much punch power on display. Both are great fighters in their own right, however putting two such styles together won't make for the most exciting of fights.

Studying the tale of the tape, both are very similar size-wise. Johnson is about twenty pounds heavier but doesn't hit as hard as, for example, Dempsey – someone who Tunney dealt with perfectly.

Johnson won't chase Tunney like Dempsey did, but rather sit back and wait for Tunney to step in range. Then he will tie him up and land uppercuts on the inside. The Fighting Marine's superior speed, stamina and activity will give him most rounds in a very anticlimactic fight.

Verdict: Decision win to Tunney.

Mike Tyson vs. Jim Jeffries

Iron Mike will come into this fight supremely confident. Even though Jeffries is tough as nails and won't back down, he simply doesn't have the size, power or technical skill to keep Kid Dynamite off him. Tyson will land some breathtaking combinations and finish Jeffries off in no time at all.

Verdict: KO win to Tyson in Round Two.

Wladimir Klitschko vs. Joe Louis

The two fighters with easily the most title defences and longest reigns in history getting it on to see who would come out on top. In one corner you have a modern super heavyweight in Dr Steelhammer Wladimir Klitschko going to war against the Brown Bomber Joe Louis, a fighter far ahead of his time and one of the greatest heavyweights in history.

Both fighters have concussive knockout power at a KO ratio of seventy-five and seventy-seven percent, respectively. Funnily enough, both are known to not have the strongest of chins, so you can guarantee someone is getting knocked out.

Louis has the slightly better chin and stamina, while Klitschko has the ring IQ and about forty pounds in weight, four inches in height and five inches in reach, which could prove to be the difference.

Once the bell rings, Louis comes forward and pushes the pace while Klitschko uses his size to control the pace and tie up Louis, leaning on him in an effort to tire him out. Pre-Emanuel Steward Klitschko would get taken apart by Louis, however this is prime Klitschko, who approaches fights from a very defensive mindset, not taking too many risks.

Louis has success with his short and powerful combinations, followed by moving out of position. He piles on the pressure early and drops Klitschko in Round Three. This gives Dr Steelhammer the shot in the arm and he starts to take more risks, letting his hands go, similar to in the Anthony Joshua fight.

Louis is susceptible to the overhand right and Klitschko has one of the best in history. In Round Five a brutal right floors Louis and tilts the fight in Klitschko's favour.

The Brown Bomber uses the minute's rest in between rounds to clear his head, however more bombs start flying his way. By Round Eight both fighters are fighting on instinct, however with the constant leaning on the smaller man, Louis starts to tire. A pulverising left hook from Klitschko causes Louis to slump onto the ropes, the ref jumping in to stop the fight.

A brilliant fight that could have gone either way between two fantastic combatants.

Verdict: TKO win to W. Klitschko in Round Eight.

Larry Holmes vs. Ken Norton

This fight happened in 1978 and was an absolute classic; possibly one of the greatest fights in history.

Verdict: Split decision win to Holmes.

Riddick Bowe vs. Floyd Patterson

Patterson isn't having the best of times in this league, and this is another mismatch for him. Big Daddy will use his superior size and inside fighting to make it virtually impossible for Patterson to have any chance.

Verdict: TKO win to Bowe in Round Four.

Co-main Event: Muhammad Ali vs. Joe Frazier

If you ask someone to name a boxing rivalry, this will be one of the first people say. Two fighters who perfectly complement each other. You have Ali – the fast talking, charismatic, arrogant, in-your-face personality – against the humble, quiet and respectful Frazier.

In the ring is no different. Ali and Frazier's styles are the perfect combination for the most dramatic, epic and beautiful trilogy of fights in history.

Looking at the fight objectively, Ali has two wins over Frazier, including a RTD win in the *Thrilla in Manila*. On the other hand, Frazier obviously has what can be argued as the single greatest win in heavyweight history with his fifteen-round decision over Ali in the *Fight of the Century*.

All things considered, you have to give the edge to Ali. Not only does he have two wins over Smokin' Joe, but he was also not in his prime when they fought. The three-year ban affected his stamina and he wasn't as fast on his feet, yet he still managed to have a great performance in the first fight, then follow it up with two wins.

Regardless of the outcome, both are magnificent fighters who gave us one of the most exciting trilogies and rivalries in history.

Verdict: Decision win to Ali.

Main Event: Jack Dempsey vs. Rocky Marciano

Ladies and gentlemen, I would like to bring your attention to perhaps the most brutal fight in heavyweight history.

Introducing first the Manassa Mauler, Jack Dempsey: known for his concussive knockout power and savagery in the ring. He is a true mean motherf*cker.

And now coming down the aisle is the Brockton Blockbuster, Rocky Marciano. Known for his iron chin, relentless stamina, body punching and pulverising power.

Please hold onto your seat, as this will be a wild, action-packed war.

Looking at the tale of the tape, Dempsey has two inches in height and six inches in reach on Marciano, though both weigh about the same. Their power is also similar, with Dempsey being the faster fighter. Where Marciano takes the edge is with his superior chin, heart, stamina and the relentless pace he sets and keeps up with throughout entire fights.

Neither fighter will have any fear of the other and will relish the opportunity to test themselves against such a worthy foe.

Once the first bell goes, Dempsey comes out flying, setting a blistering pace and throwing all sorts of punches, completely overwhelming the Rock with his speed and savage attacks. Marciano always starts slow and prefers to work his way into a fight. The destructive Dempsey is fully aware of this and looks to end the fight as early as possible.

In mid-Round One a poleaxing left hook sends Marciano down. With the ref at seven, Marciano rises and is now seriously pissed.

The crowd is on their feet, sensing an early stoppage, and Dempsey is more than happy to oblige. He comes charging in, throwing menacing punches with both fists. However Marciano holds and sees out a rough opening round.

In between rounds, the Rock can be seen smiling at Dempsey, giving him a knowing look as if to say, "Why don't you try that again?"

Round Two begins similarly to the first, with Dempsey piling on the pressure and opening up cuts on Marciano's face. Marciano knows not to stay too long in the pocket and starts to push Dempsey back while working over his body and landing some big shots of his own.

By Round Three Marciano has fully settled into the fight and lands a perfect Suzie Q, sending Dempsey to the canvas. Dempsey is not too hurt and gets to his feet, knowing he's in for one hell of a war.

By Round Four Dempsey's left eye is starting to swell, but he still has plenty in the tank. He starts to use his speed and slashing punches to cut up Marciano's face. Blood is now pouring from multiple cuts across his face and the canvas is covered with blotches of red. All the while, the crowd is at fever pitch.

Tasting his blood drives the Brockton Blockbuster onward and he comes out full force in Round Six, landing some seriously draining body punches.

Dempsey knows he can't let the contest go on much longer, otherwise the relentless Marciano will run away with the fight. He comes out for the seventh round and throws everything at his enemy, really busting him open. Marciano doesn't take one backwards step and keeps pushing forward, however with his slow speed and lack of defence, Dempsey's bombs are making things look ominous.

By Round Eight, both look like they have been in a car crash. The ref has seen enough and as soon as Dempsey starts landing with his combinations, he steps in and calls off the fight.

This is the heavyweight version of Hagler vs. Hearns.

Verdict: TKO win to Dempsey in Eight.

Summary: Fight Cards One to Five

S o, with the first five fight cards done, how are things shaping up? Looking at the league standings below you have three fighters undefeated in Lewis, Ali and Tyson, plus three fighters yet to score a win in Jeffries, Patterson and Johnson.

For some, the fights have been a bit unfavourable. For instance, Holyfield – who is two-three – has had some tough matchups, and even his losses were extremely close fights that could have gone either way. I imagine the next five fights will be very different for the Real Deal.

Of the three undefeated fighters, Lewis and Ali have had a relatively easy start with the only real threats Ali faced in Holmes and W. Klitschko. For Lewis, he was still the clear favourite going into his most difficult fights against Liston and Frazier.

Tyson has had two stand-out wins over tough competition in Louis and Bowe, but this is coupled with three very favourable stylistic fights against Johnson, Norton and Jeffries.

We have already witnessed some truly incredible fights, with some of the standouts so far being:

- Evander Holyfield vs. Joe Frazier
- Mike Tyson vs. Riddick Bowe
- Rocky Marciano vs. Evander Holyfield
- George Foreman vs. Joe Louis
- Joe Louis vs. Mike Tyson

- Jack Dempsey vs. Rocky Marciano (This one fight fans will be discussing for years to come; easily the best fight so far.)

Current League Standings After Five Fight Cards

		Wins	Losses	Draws	Points
1	Lennox Lewis	5			15
2	Mike Tyson	5			15
3	Muhammad Ali	5			15
4	George Foreman	4	1		12
5	Larry Holmes	4	1		12
6	Vitali Klitschko	4	1		12
7	Jack Dempsey	3	2		9
8	Joe Louis	3	2		9
9	Riddick Bowe	3	2		9
10	Sonny Liston	3	2		9
11	Wladimir Klitschko	3	2		9
12	Evander Holyfield	2	3		6
13	Gene Tunney	2	3		6
14	Joe Frazier	1	4		3
15	Ken Norton	1	4		3
16	Max Schmeling	1	4		3
17	Rocky Marciano	1	4		3

18	Floyd Patterson		5		0
19	Jack Johnson		5		0
20	Jim Jeffries		5		0

Only one fighter was undefeated his whole career on this list, and that was Rocky Marciano. There is no way any fighter will remain undefeated against the other nineteen fighters all in their primes, so there will be losses suffered for all.

Let's see how the next five fight cards play out.

FIGHT CARD SIX

Evander Holyfield vs. Jack Dempsey

Lennox Lewis vs. Vitali Klitschko

Max Schmeling vs. Mike Tyson

Jim Jeffries vs. Wladimir Klitschko

Joe Louis vs. Larry Holmes

Joe Frazier vs. Riddick Bowe

Ken Norton vs. Gene Tunney

Floyd Patterson vs. Jack Johnson

Co-main Event: Sonny Liston vs. George Foreman

Main Event: Rocky Marciano vs. Muhammad Ali

Evander Holyfield vs. Jack Dempsey

Kicking off our next round of fights is another instant classic between two warriors not afraid to mix it up.

Comparing the two fighters shows that Holyfield is one-and-a-half inches taller with an extra four-and-a-half inches in reach and about twenty pounds in weight. This will encourage Holyfield to go to war. Not the best of strategies, but the fans won't be complaining.

Dempsey is clearly the harder hitter and the faster of the two, while Holyfield has the edge with much better boxing skills, size and ring IQ.

A real toss up of a fight that could end at any point if Dempsey lands flush and catches Holyfield off guard. If Holyfield simply sticks to his boxing and countering he could win a twelve-round decision, however that is a big if.

Will Holyfield be able to resist trading with such a tough and aggressive fighter who is smaller than him? I doubt it. The Real Deal will have a point to prove and want to show off his gigantic heart.

As predicted, the first round is Dempsey coming out and looking for a brutal quick finish. Holyfield is prepared and uses his skills and size to avoid the most damaging of punches, frustrating Dempsey.

After a few rounds Holyfield is up on all the judges and is feeling pretty confident. He starts letting his hands go a bit too much and stays on the inside for a little too long. Dempsey sees the opportunity and starts to turn up the heat, landing some vicious punches, hurting Holyfield and dropping him in Round Six. With Holyfield's great chin he gets up and rides out the Category Five storm.

As the Real Deal settles back into his boxing, he starts to land some beautiful combinations that stun his opponent, with the Manassa Mauler now realising he needs a knockout. The championship rounds consist of him wildly chasing down Holyfield and looking to finish him off.

With Holyfield's superior skills he has already made the adjustments necessary to avoid the clinch and fighting on the inside, making Dempsey less dangerous and unable to find the knockout.

Verdict: Decision win to Holyfield.

Lennox Lewis vs. Vitali Klitschko

This fight, known as *TKO6*, happened in 2003, with Lewis winning on cuts in Round Six.

Even though Klitschko was ahead, Lewis was getting back into the fight and was starting to find his range, landing some real heavy shots. Lewis was clearly not in the best shape and was gassing quite hard, but he still managed to get the win and that's all that really matters.

Verdict: TKO win to Lewis in Round Six.

Max Schmeling vs. Mike Tyson

Schmeling will be too slow and easy to hit to take Tyson into the latter rounds. This will be a one-sided annihilation.

Verdict: KO win to Tyson in Round Two.

Jim Jeffries vs. Wladimir Klitschko

Jeffries is just too small and doesn't have enough pop in his punches to worry Klitschko. Klitschko will not come barging in and take his time for the first two or three rounds, but ultimately he is bigger, hits harder and has superior boxing skills. Another one-sided fight.

Verdict: TKO win to W. Klitschko in Round Five.

Joe Louis vs. Larry Holmes

Now this will be some fight. You have Louis' great power and combination punching as well as fast hands against Holmes' great technical skills, formidable jab, fast hands and feet. This is a real pick 'em fight that could go either way.

Holmes has one inch in height, five inches in reach and about twenty pounds of muscle on Louis. While Louis is clearly the harder hitter and better finisher with a seventy-five percent KO ratio compared to Holmes' fifty-nine.

The fight is on a razor's edge the entire time. The first few rounds consist of Holmes trying to keep the fight technical, establishing the jab and following up with hooks while using his lateral movement to avoid Louis' most devastating punches.

Louis is trying to drag Holmes into a brawl, aiming to hurt him and look for a quick finish. Holmes knows he needs to box very strategically and avoid taking too many unnecessary chances.

By Round Six, Louis is behind on the cards but isn't too worried as he can see Holmes starting to slow and inevitably staying in range for a little too long. Louis pounces and knocks Holmes down with a great right hand.

Even though Holmes can survive hits from great punchers like Shavers, Louis has great tenacity to finish off opponents and turns up the pressure with great eye-catching punches that cause Holmes to stagger into the ropes. The ref has no choice but to waive it off.

Verdict: TKO win to Louis in Round Seven.

Joe Frazier vs. Riddick Bowe

This fight could be fought in a telephone booth. Both are great fighters who prefer to fight on the inside and not take a backward step.

Even though Bowe is much bigger at six inches taller, eight inches further in reach and twenty pounds heavier, Frazier fights at a relentless pace and has the heart of a lion. He will easily be Bowe's hardest-hitting opponent to date. Neither fighter will be the same after such a gruelling fight.

The fight starts at a fast pace with Frazier coming out of the gates and taking it straight to Bowe, landing some great body shots and following them up with hooks to the chin.

Having felt Frazier's power, Bowe knows he's in for a tough night's work and starts using his jab and uppercuts when Frazier comes in, then starts to lean on him, trying to sap Frazier's legs of energy. Smokin' Joe is prepared for this and moves to the side to avoid clinching too much.

In Round Five Bowe throws his trademark looping right hand, however Frazier has done his homework and counters with a perfectly timed left hook that sends Bowe crashing to the canvas.

Throughout each round Bowe lands some great flush shots, however he just doesn't have enough force in his punches to really hurt Frazier like Foreman did. Big Daddy is also pretty easy to hit and allows himself to get involved in too many exchanges.

After twelve long and gruelling rounds, Frazier's relentless work rate is enough to give him the nod.

Verdict: Decision win to Frazier.

Ken Norton vs. Gene Tunney

This will be an interesting fight with Tunney using his speed and skills to keep moving and fighting on the outside. Meanwhile Norton will look to close the distance and use his awkward style to frustrate Tunney and utilise his size to land some heavy shots. Both fighters have great stamina and don't hit that hard, so you can imagine this going the full twelve rounds.

Overall Norton's awkward style and simply being the bigger fighter will make it very difficult for Tunney to have any real sustained success. If Norton could beat a six feet three inch Ali who was faster and bigger than Tunney and have a razor-close loss to Holmes, he should have enough in the tank to get the win over the Fighting Marine.

Verdict: Decision win to Norton.

Floyd Patterson vs. Jack Johnson

Patterson's biggest weakness is his chin, which just doesn't hold up to heavy hitters. Johnson, on the other hand, isn't a power puncher and relies on his defensive skills to control fights and wear opponents down.

Johnson has the lowest KO ratio on this list at only forty percent and is much slower than Patterson, who could match Ali in terms of speed.

Patterson will simply outbox and avoid Johnson's punches, keeping the fight at a distance. Johnson has never faced anyone with such a speed advantage over him and just doesn't have the tools or style to hurt or finish off Patterson.

Verdict: Decision win to Patterson.

Co-main Event: Sonny Liston vs. George Foreman

This will be one of the most brutal and heart-stopping fights in history, with two of the most intimidating men to ever set foot in the ring going toe to toe. This has *fireworks* written all over it.

Looking at the tale of the tape, Foreman is three inches taller, Liston has the longer reach at eighty-four inches, and both weigh about the same. Foreman has the slight speed and heart advantage with Liston having better stamina and boxing skills. The power on display in this fight will be spectacular, as both hit like freight trucks.

The fight begins with the iciest stare down in history. Neither fighter blinks, looks away or shows any sign of weakness. A lesser man would be frozen in place, but not these two. Both come in full of confidence and belief that they have the tools to knock the other out. This fight is definitely not going the distance.

Once the bell rings Foreman comes out and tries to finish off Liston early, but he weathers the early onslaught pretty comfortably and lands some stinging left jabs of his own, stopping Foreman in his tracks.

In Round Two Big George lands his walking left jab/hook bang on the money and sends Liston down for the count. Liston gets up, shakes his head and waves Foreman in. Foreman comes in for the finish, however Liston isn't hurt, just annoyed at getting caught. He starts to use his own brute strength to push Foreman back and land some flush shots of his own.

Foreman has a very distinct tactic of pushing his opponents back with his arms to take them off balance, however this doesn't work against Liston, who's just as strong (if not stronger) and possesses a longer reach.

Most rounds consist of Liston landing his jab and following it up with some strong right hands to wear Big George out.

By Round Six, Liston is tiring. However Foreman is completely shattered. The Big Bear's better stamina and superior boxing skills have allowed him to pace himself better, and when he sees Foreman breathing heavily he starts raining down huge right hands and short hooks to knock him down.

By Round Eight Foreman is hanging on for life and has completely emptied his tank. Liston has enough left to land a powerful one-two, sending Foreman down for the count one final time.

Verdict: KO win to Liston in Round Eight.

Main Event: Rocky Marciano vs. Muhammad Ali

Now this is a fight that boxing aficionados have been discussing since Ali burst onto the scene. You have the dominant fighter of the fifties going up against the dominant fighter of the sixties and seventies.

This will be a real clash of styles. Marciano is the come-forward brawler with an iron chin, power, stamina to spare and relentless body punches. This is versus the speed and reflexes of Ali as well as his ring craft, superhuman endurance and huge heart. This will be one great fight that the whole world will stop to witness.

An interesting bit of trivia is this fight actually happened in 1969 as part of a match decided by computer simulation known as *The Super Fight*. Numerous endings were filmed, but the one that was settled on was a TKO win to Marciano. Ali did comment that Marciano hit very hard, however this was clearly not a real fight and Ali only participated during his ban for financial reasons, so the result should be taken with caution.

Now, how do they stack up against each other?

Ali is the bigger man with a five-inch height, eleven-inch reach and thirty-pound weight advantage. Ali is also by far the faster and better boxer, based on past performances. Marciano has the stronger chin, but not by a lot.

One thing that is generally agreed is that Foreman, Liston and Shavers all hit harder than Marciano, and Ali took their best shots and didn't go down. The Rock will have to set a relentless pace, attacking the body and whipping some great overhand rights while Ali is pinned against the ropes.

Ali's best strategy will be to keep the fight at a distance and use his speed and size to frustrate and nullify Marciano's attacks. One thing to consider is Ali doesn't have the power to outright stop Marciano early like Foreman or Tyson would.

As soon as the first bell rings Marciano comes out like a bull, throwing powerful shots to the body and whipping punches to Ali's chin.

The Greatest is fully prepared for this and uses his speed to avoid Marciano while landing his fast combinations directly on target. The Rock did have a tendency to block punches with his face, and Ali is more than willing to oblige, throwing slashing punches from all angles and opening up cuts over both of Marciano's eyes.

By Round Six the Brockton Bomber's face is a complete mess and Ali is still going strong with no sign of letting up.

During Round Eight Marciano finally has Ali in some serious trouble and he lands his trademark Suzie Q.

Ali is rocked. With a dazed look coming over his eyes, he pivots out of position while shaking his head, signalling that the blow didn't hurt. Both he and his opponent know it did in fact hurt, and while Ali is acting composed and unaffected, internally he chides himself for being hit so cleanly.

Marciano is spurred on and burrows into his opponent's chest, firing a left to the body, right to the head and another left to Ali's ribs. Ali is holding on but is starting to feel the effects of such unrelenting attacks. However, Marciano is unable to finish him off and the bell sounds, giving Ali a much needed reprieve.

The minute-long break is enough time for Ali to recover and he comes out for the ninth with a point to prove. Triggering his jab and will and following it up with dazzling three-four punch combinations, Ali is back in command and has the bit between his teeth.

By Round Ten Ali has completely taken over the fight and it is literally target practice with Marciano's face totally cut up and covered in blood. The doctor calls off the fight in Round Eleven, much to Marciano's vehement protests.

Verdict: TKO win to Ali in Round Eleven.

FIGHT CARD SEVEN

Vitali Klitschko vs. Sonny Liston

Jack Dempsey vs. Lennox Lewis

Floyd Patterson vs. Ken Norton

Wladimir Klitschko vs. Max Schmeling

Jack Johnson vs. Joe Frazier

Larry Holmes vs. Jim Jeffries

Riddick Bowe vs. Rocky Marciano

Gene Tunney vs. Joe Louis

Co-main Event: Muhammad Ali vs. Evander Holyfield

Main Event: Mike Tyson vs. George Foreman

Vitali Klitschko vs. Sonny Liston

This will be a pretty rough fight to watch. Both men hit hard and have durable chins. Liston will be giving up a lot of size, being six inches shorter and forty pounds lighter, but bizarrely having four inches in reach over Klitschko.

Will the size difference be too much for Liston to overcome? Not necessarily, however Klitschko has an iron chin and won't have an issue with the fight going into deep waters.

Overall, with his massive size, iron chin and powerful punches, Klitschko will be too much for the Big Bear to conquer.

Verdict: TKO win to V. Klitschko in Round Ten.

Jack Dempsey vs. Lennox Lewis

Dempsey certainly has the power and speed to hurt Lewis, but again the huge size difference and the fact that Lewis is the more technical and smarter fighter won't give Dempsey much of a chance.

Verdict: KO win to Lewis in Round Four.

Floyd Patterson vs. Ken Norton

An interesting fight, since neither fighter has the strongest of chins and both have great gas tanks. You can expect a long, drawn-out fight, with Patterson's speed and technical skills going against Norton's awkward cross guard, great stamina and toughness.

Both have similar power with sixty-three and sixty-six percent KO ratios, respectively. A common opponent is Ali, and a lot can be drawn from these fights. Ali easily handled Patterson twice, however struggled three times with Norton, losing once.

The fight starts with Patterson using his speed and combination punches to keep Norton at bay and rack up the early rounds.

During the middle of the fight Norton's body punches begin to slow Patterson down and the Jawbreaker comes on strong for the second half of the fight.

This is a very evenly contested fight, however two things make the difference for the winner. Firstly, Norton's size advantage with four inches in height, twenty pounds in weight and ten inches in reach, as well as his superior conditioning. Norton does not tire. In fact, Patterson hangs on to the final bell, having suffered a bruising final six rounds.

Verdict: Split decision win to Norton.

Wladimir Klitschko vs. Max Schmeling

A routine win for Klitschko. Sadly for Schmeling he has nothing in his locker that would even trouble the Ukrainian.

Verdict: KO win to W. Klitschko in Round Three.

Jack Johnson vs. Joe Frazier

This fight will be entirely fought on the inside, where both men are most comfortable. Johnson's defensive skills will make him a difficult target to hit, and he will tie up Frazier on the inside, frustrating him and throwing him off his rhythm. Frazier will come forward relentlessly and attack the body, relying on his left hook to cause some serious damage.

Both fighters are virtually the same size, though Johnson is an inch-and-a-half taller, has half an inch of reach advantage and is four pounds heavier than Frazier.

The fight starts in Johnson's favour, with him controlling the pace and landing some good clean shots on Frazier's chin.

Frazier tends to start slow, picking up momentum as the rounds progress. From Round Four he cranks up the intensity, working over Johnson's body and putting him under significant pressure.

By Round Twelve the judges have Frazier ahead by a couple of rounds. Sensing this, Johnson comes out looking for the finish. This falls right into Frazier's game plan, enabling him to land a crushing left hook that drops Johnson to the canvas.

The Galveston Giant bravely rises at the count of seven, but is groggy and tired. Undeterred, Johnson still looks to end the fight, however with a forty percent KO ratio and being worn down by Frazier's attacks, Johnson just doesn't have it in him to force the stoppage.

Verdict: Decision win to Frazier.

Larry Holmes vs. Jim Jeffries

Both fighters are very evenly matched in size, however there is a massive gulf in boxing skills and speed – all in favour of Holmes. This will be an easy twelve-round decision win to Holmes, who will simply outbox Jeffries.

Verdict: Decision win to Holmes.

Riddick Bowe vs. Rocky Marciano

This card has had quite a few one-sided affairs, and this is no different.

Marciano loves to make it a tough fight, keeping the bout on the inside and roughing up his opponents. The problem with this strategy is that, simply put, Bowe is one of the best inside fighters in the history of the division. Coupled with the big size difference, it will make Marciano's job virtually impossible.

Verdict: TKO win to Bowe in Round Seven.

Gene Tunney vs. Joe Louis

Now we have a genuine clash of styles, with both fighters having completely different approaches to the other to etch out the win.

Tunney has no issue with stinking out a fight if he is ahead and is very defensive against powerful punchers, such as in the Dempsey fight. Louis has just as much power and throws some blistering combinations, so it's fair to assume that Tunney will employ a similar tactic in this fight.

Both fighters are virtually the same size, with the only advantage being two inches in height in favour of Louis. Louis is by far the harder hitter and better finisher, with Tunney having the advantage in footwork and ring IQ. Louis has fast hands but slow feet and doesn't like to move his head, so he won't be too hard to hit.

The fight starts with Tunney sticking and moving, exploiting some defensive weak points in Louis' skills. For large parts of the early rounds, Louis is stalking Tunney, goading him to come forward and engage, however the Fighting Marine is too smart to fall for this and sticks to his game plan perfectly.

By the mid rounds Louis is starting to get frustrated with his lack of success and the crowd is growing restless, with some boos being directed at Tunney.

Coming into the championship rounds, Tunney is starting to slow a little and Louis finally sees his chance, with Tunney staying in range a little too long. A crushing left hook followed up with some powerful rights and lefts sends him to the canvas.

He rises at nine, but on rubbery legs, and Louis goes in for the kill. A powerful right to the temple finishes the job.

Verdict: TKO win to Louis in Round Eleven.

Co-main Event: Muhammad Ali vs. Evander Holyfield

This will be one hell of a battle; two great warriors with huge hearts, not afraid to take on anyone, going head to head.

I would argue that they have the two greatest resumes in history, having fought numerous all-time great fighters in their primes. From this book alone, Ali's list of foes reads like a murderer's row: Frazier, Foreman, Liston, Norton, Patterson and Holmes, with him going nine wins and three losses. Holyfield's resume is almost as great, with names such as Foreman, Bowe, Tyson, Lewis and Holmes, with five wins, three losses and one draw against such opposition.

Examining the tale of tape, both fighters are virtually the same size. Holyfield is the more skilled fighter with great fundamentals and superior inside fighting. Neither are known for their KO power, but I would give the edge to Ali in terms of who hits the hardest. However with both possessing great chins and endurance, this fight is definitely not ending early.

Ali has all his usual advantages of sublime speed with both hand and feet, ring IQ and an ability to string together some beautiful combinations and move out of range within a matter of seconds. Both fighters will be fully respectful and wary of their opponent, not taking such a crucial fight lightly.

As soon as the first bell rings, Ali comes out light on his feet, moving around and throwing the left jab and circling Holyfield. When he spots an opening, he steps in range, fires off three or four quick shots and then is gone like the wind.

Holyfield gives Ali issues with his stiff jab and great conditioning, however he has a tendency to engage too easily and doing so against an adversary with such an advantage in hand speed is not the best of strategies.

The Real Deal has his moments in the fight and lands some great shots, however he can't hit hard enough to truly worry the Greatest. Ali's activity, movement and reflexes would see him win a hard fought but comfortable twelve-round decision.

Verdict: Decision win to Ali.

Main Event: Mike Tyson vs. George Foreman

A fight that will easily be one of the biggest in boxing history. Both have fan-friendly styles and are aggressive, powerful and always looking for the finish.

It is a shame this fight didn't happen in the nineties, as Foreman specifically came back to fight Tyson, but it never came to fruition. We're here to compare the prime version of Foreman, who dismantled Frazier in two, and the prime version of Tyson who took out Spinks in ninety seconds.

How do both of these warriors stack up against each other?

Foreman is the bigger fighter, with six inches in height and eight inches in reach over Tyson. Both weigh the same though, given Tyson's tank-like build.

Comparing power, you have two of the hardest hitters in history. Foreman has brute force and devastating KO power, perhaps the hardest hitter in this book. Tyson has great speed, explosiveness and dynamite in both fists, however on balance Foreman hits slightly harder and is definitely stronger.

Foreman also has the tougher chin, whereas Tyson excels in speed, defensive skills and combination punching.

Both fighters are very evenly matched, and this could go either way.

As the ref gives his instructions, neither fighter takes their eyes off the other. Both come into the fight supremely confident and the build-up got heated with both declaring they would knock the other out.

Foreman stares straight into Tyson's soul with those cold, dark eyes and a deep scowl on his face.

Tyson is not giving anything up, staring right back, thinking to himself, I'm going to knock you the f*ck out.

Two caged animals ready to tear each other apart, piece by piece.

The first bell rings and we are off. The commentators are urging people to hold their breath as fireworks are about to go off.

Tyson comes out of his corner and doesn't waste any time throwing rights and lefts, using his great footwork and speed to bob and weave in and out of position while letting off some great body and head shots.

Foreman isn't too concerned and was expecting a fast start from his foe. What he is surprised by is Tyson's speed and elusiveness. Also, his shots are hurting when they land. Foreman weathers the early onslaught and starts to push Tyson back, landing some hard jabs of his own during the second half of Round One.

Round Two begins and both fighters have settled into the fight and know exactly what they are dealing with. Things start a little quiet and then, out of nowhere, Tyson lands a perfectly-timed body shot then follows it up with a huge left hook to the temple.

Foreman is down. The ref jumps in and has to push Tyson into the neutral corner. The count is at five when Foreman rises.

Tyson comes gunning in and throws the kitchen sink at his adversary, looking for a quick end to his night's work.

Unfortunately, Foreman is too experienced and survives a rough round.

Round Three starts the same, with Tyson looking to take Foreman out. However Foreman has used the minute's rest to clear his head and make some adjustments to avoid the combinations of Tyson as best he can.

With Tyson controlling the pace and landing some nice strikes, he walks straight into Foreman's missile right hand and it sends Tyson to the ropes. However, he manages to hold on and see out the round.

Round Four and Tyson is starting to slow. Foreman uses his strength and size to start pushing Tyson back, throwing some of his own brutal blows.

Tyson can take the shots but is struggling to fight going back and hasn't got any way to deal with Foreman's freakish strength. Foreman's heavy blows are starting to take a toll on the smaller fighter and, when up close, Foreman ties him up and starts to lean on him, sapping Tyson of some much needed energy.

By Round Five Tyson is starting to feel frustrated and suffers his worst round yet, with Foreman coming on strong and punishing him when he comes in. Foreman has a great ability to make his opponent fight at the range he prefers and is taking full advantage of his tiring foe.

Round Six and Tyson is looking pretty dejected, but his warrior attitude won't let him give up. He comes out and starts throwing everything at Foreman. With Foreman's adjustments he is able to parry most of the punches and the ones that land are absorbed by his granite chin.

In Round Seven Foreman senses the end is near. He comes on strong, pushing Tyson back relentlessly and throwing jabs, hooks and overhand rights. Tyson is now hanging on and just doesn't have enough to turn this around.

Big George lands a vicious right on Tyson's chin and he's down for the count. Tyson bravely gets up, but with his eyes glazed over the ref calls it off.

Verdict: TKO win to Foreman in Round Seven.

FIGHT CARD EIGHT

Jack Dempsey vs. Sonny Liston

Wladimir Klitschko vs. Mike Tyson

Ken Norton vs. Rocky Marciano

Muhammad Ali vs. Vitali Klitschko

Larry Holmes vs. George Foreman

Gene Tunney vs. Max Schmeling

Jack Johnson vs. Evander Holyfield

Floyd Patterson vs. Jim Jeffries

Co-main Event: Joe Frazier vs. Joe Louis

Main Event: Riddick Bowe vs. Lennox Lewis

Jack Dempsey vs. Sonny Liston

The first contest to kick off Fight Card Eight is a brutal affair that pits the Manassa Mauler against the Big Bear, two fighters known for their devastating punching power and clinical finishing. Both fighters love to tear through their opponents like a buzzsaw and this will be violent for as long as it lasts.

Looking at the tale of the tape, they are both six-feet-one, however Liston has about twenty pounds of weight and a massive eleven-inch reach advantage.

The power on display will be phenomenal. Liston hits the harder of the two and is definitely stronger, however he is also slower and Dempsey has great speed and quickness and is able to throw some sublime combinations when up close. A real pick 'em of a fight that will hang in the balance from the first bell.

At the start of the fight Dempsey comes straight out and puts it on Liston, throwing all sorts of punches looking to hurt and finish off his foe. Dempsey loves attacking bigger fighters and has no hesitation going in for the kill. Whenever Dempsey is fearful or wary of his opponents, as he certainly is of Liston, it somehow makes him deadlier than usual; a real "kill or be killed" attitude.

Liston weathers the early storm and by Round Two is using his ramrod jab and better boxing skills to control the pace and keep Dempsey at bay. Dempsey is having serious issues with the reach advantage and whenever he manages to get up close Liston ties him and uses his vast strength advantage to bully and push the smaller man around the ring.

By Round Five Dempsey is becoming very frustrated with his lack of success and turns up the heat, looking to land hurtful shots on the Big Bear. He walks straight into a huge uppercut and is knocked down.

Dempsey is not too hurt and gets to his feet with a few seconds to spare. Now he is really pissed off and wants to literally tear Liston's head off. However, Liston is prepared and lands a perfect right hook, knocking his rival down for the count.

Verdict: KO win to Liston in Round Five.

Wladimir Klitschko vs. Mike Tyson

Even though Klitschko has a massive size advantage, Tyson is faster, more explosive and can be hard to hit with his bob and weave style and good footwork. Klitschko doesn't have the sturdiest of chins and will definitely get tagged by Tyson's initial onslaught. Once this happens his composure will go, and it will be a quick finish.

Verdict: TKO win to Tyson in Round Three.

Ken Norton vs. Rocky Marciano

Similar to the last fight, Norton has the size and reach advantage however can't deal with hard hitters, and Marciano will throw some deadly bombs. Norton will come in trying to tie up the Rock and push him around, however Marciano's relentless body attacks and hooks to the head will be too much for Norton to handle.

Verdict: KO win to Marciano in Round Five.

Muhammad Ali vs. Vitali Klitschko

The endurance on display in this fight will be incredible; both have almost superhuman chins and will not stop fighting, so expect this to go the distance.

Ali has speed, skills, stamina and ring IQ in his favour, whereas Klitschko is much bigger by four inches in height and about thirty-five pounds of weight, though only two inches in reach. He also hits harder and, on balance, has a stronger chin.

On paper this will be a pretty close fight and if Klitschko can force Ali to fight his fight, he could have a real chance at winning.

However, in reality, the biggest deciding factor is speed. Ali is insanely fast with both hands and feet and Klitschko is slow and robotic. Also, Dr Ironfist can't fight on the inside, so even if he manages to tie up the smaller fighter, he won't have the ability to take advantage.

Furthermore, Ali is too smart a fighter to let this fight become a brawl and will be very aware of his opponent's power. Ali will dance around just out of range and cut Klitschko up in ribbons with his fast-slashing punches. By the end of the fight Klitschko's face will be similar to in the Lewis fight.

Verdict: Decision win to Ali.

Larry Holmes vs. George Foreman

A true clash of styles with the silky-smooth skills and movement of Holmes going up against the rough and hard-hitting Foreman. This fight could have happened in the seventies and nineties, but sadly never came to fruition.

Both fighters are virtually the same size. Foreman hits harder and has the stronger chin, while Holmes is the better and faster boxer with superior stamina and ring IQ.

The fight starts with Holmes fully aware of Big George's power and early rushing attacks. Holmes whips his incredible jab and tries to control the pace, aiming to manoeuvre the predatory Foreman into positions where he can't land his power punches. Adopting the rope a dope wouldn't be a smart idea as Holmes doesn't have the endurance or chin that Ali did, and it would be a very risky strategy.

After a few rounds Holmes is up on the cards, but Foreman isn't too worried as he is landing some glancing blows and isn't working to such a pace as he did in the Rumble in the Jungle *when Ali constantly taunted him.*

Holmes also doesn't hit hard enough to really hurt or worry his foe and also had a tendency to carry his hands low and trade with punches unnecessarily, like against Shavers and Norton. A pretty bad idea against an all-time great puncher and finisher like Big George.

By Seven Holmes switches off and Foreman lands a devastating left hook on his chin. Holmes is down. The Easton Assassin gets to his feet but an on-rushing Foreman starts teeing off with some clubbing shots and the ref jumps in, ending the contest.

Verdict: TKO win to Foreman in Round Seven.

Gene Tunney vs. Max Schmeling

Schmeling has some great early successes with his big overhand right, stunning Tunney a couple of times during the first four rounds. However, Tunney is too smart a fighter and makes some adjustments, using his jab to control the tempo of the fight and his superior hand and foot speed to avoid Schmeling's attacks.

The Fighting Marine rides out an unspectacular twelve-round decision.

Verdict: Decision win to Tunney.

Jack Johnson vs. Evander Holyfield

This isn't a very good stylistic match for Johnson; Holyfield is too active, hits harder and has the better chin, as well as being bigger. It won't be an exciting fight and Johnson will have no way to deal with such a polished fighter as the Real Deal.

Verdict: Decision to Holyfield.

Floyd Patterson vs. Jim Jeffries

This fight has Patterson, the faster and more skilled boxer, going head to head with the bigger, stronger puncher in Jeffries. A classic boxer versus puncher showdown.

Jeffries is quite a bit bigger by two-and-a-half inches in height, thirty-seven pounds in weight and seven inches in reach.

Patterson starts fast and uses his speed and skills to fluster Jeffries, landing some very flashy shots and racking up the rounds early on.

As the rounds wear on, Patterson is slowing down and Jeffries' punches and strength are starting to have an effect. One of Patterson's biggest weaknesses is a hard left to the body, which just so happens to be his opponent's best punch.

As expected, in Round Eight Jeffries lands a crunching left to the body that takes the wind and fight right out of Patterson. Patterson is down and can't get back to his feet in time.

Verdict: KO win to Jeffries in Round Eight.

Co-main Event: Joe Frazier vs. Joe Louis

What an incredible fight we now have for our co-main event. In the blue corner, hailing from Alabama, USA is the Brown Bomber, Joe Louis. And in the red corner from South Carolina, USA is Smokin' Joe Frazier.

Analysing the tale of the tape shows Frazier as the heavier fighter by eleven pounds and Louis having the longer reach by two-and-a-half inches, and also the height advantage, being three inches taller.

Louis is clearly the harder hitter with better combinations, and Frazier has the heart and work rate in his favour, as well as his show-stopping left hook. An evenly matched contest that could go either way.

Ringside commentators are buzzing for such a fantastic matchup, with opinions on the winner split right down the middle. Some argue Louis' combination punching and power is too much to handle for Frazier, while others respond that Smokin' Joe's relentless pressure and heart will grind down Louis over a long and tough fight.

One way or another, the audience is at fever pitch and can't wait for the first bell.

The sound of the first bell echoes throughout the arena and the fight is on. Frazier comes forward and starts eating some beautiful combinations to the head, already looking a bit shaky. The Brown Bomber piles on the pressure and towards the end of the first round knocks Frazier down with a great one-two. Smokin' Joe beats the count, and the bell sounds to signal the end of the round.

In between rounds Frazier's corner are pleading with him to start faster this round and stop fighting to Louis' strengths.

The second round begins, and Louis is feeling pretty confident, still landing his jab and following it up with some great two-three punch combinations. Frazier is starting to get a little frustrated and towards the end of the round lands a great left hook, which stuns his opponent. But the bell rings before any further damage can be inflicted.

Round Three and Frazier comes storming off his stool, however Louis has recovered and starts to take over the round with Frazier walking into too many shots and not getting off any of his own. Sensing the round slipping away, Frazier charges forward but gets tagged and is down again. This time it's more of a flash knockdown, and he manages to clear his head and see out the round.

Round Four and Louis is starting to settle into the fight, feeling confident. Everything is going to plan, however a niggling sense at the back of his mind is telling him things are about to get a whole lot worse. Frazier is starting to get stronger as the fight continues and doesn't ever seem to take a backwards step. Louis is very impressed with his foe, but still controls most of the round, stringing together some nice punches.

Rounds Five to Seven consist of Frazier pushing Louis up against the ropes and working over his body, landing some tough hooks and right hands to the head. Frazier's pressure is starting to wear the Brown Bomber down and tiredness is starting to set in.

Rounds Eight to Ten are mainly Louis throwing some great shots while Frazier is coming in. Once inside, Smokin' Joe lets his brutal shots go, really working over Louis' body.

One of the Brown Bomber's biggest weaknesses is his slow feet and lack of head movement, and with the fight entering the championship rounds, he's feeling the effects of such a long and tough fight. The early work Frazier put into the body is starting to pay dividends.

Round Eleven and Frazier lands his leaping left hook bang on the chin and Louis is down for the count. He bravely rises but is on wobbly legs. For the first time in his career, Louis sees the look an onrushing bull has when faced with the colour red.

Frazier rushes in and starts to pile on the pressure, sensing the end is near. Another left hook sends Louis falling into the corner and the ref has finally seen enough, stepping in to end the fight and save Louis from further punishment.

The audience are on their feet and clapping at such an amazing display from both fighters. An instant classic.

Verdict: TKO win to Frazier in Round Eleven.

Main Event: Riddick Bowe vs. Lennox Lewis

The fight that never was. Both were at their peaks in the nineties and a fight between the two would have been nothing short of spectacular.

The two share quite a bit of history, with Lewis first approaching Bowe at the Olympics and declaring that he would knock him out, then subsequently doing so in the final to win gold.

In the pro ranks, Bowe was the WBC champion and opted to literally throw his belt into the trash rather than fight his mandatory challenger Lewis in 1992. The fight was signed later on, however Lewis suffered a shocking KO loss to Oliver McCall, which derailed plans. A real shame, as it would have been one hell of a showdown.

So how do both superheavyweights stack up? In a nutshell, very evenly. Both are six feet six inches, though Lewis has three inches in reach and about fourteen pounds in weight over Bowe.

Stylistically it will be a tremendous fight. Both hit extremely hard with a seventy-two and seventy-three percent KO ratio, respectively. On balance, I would probably give Lewis the slight edge in power as he has knocked out better opposition.

In terms of speed, they are about the same. Bowe has the stronger chin, and Lewis the slightly better heart and ring IQ.

We are literally talking fine margins and I'd be surprised if there is a better-balanced fight in this book.

Bowe likes to fight on the inside and land hard jabs and uppercuts, while Lewis prefers to keep things at a distance and land his sledgehammer right. I won't be surprised if this fight ends in a double KO like in the *Street Fighter* computer game.

With Steward in his corner, Lewis comes into this fight sharp and ready with the perfect game plan. Bowe is aware of this and expects him to be one of, if not the *toughest opponent he will ever face, wanting to exact revenge on his loss in the 1988 final. He arrives in the shape of his life.*

The fight starts tentatively, with both feeling each other out and not wanting to take too many risks early on.

The second round starts, with Bowe catching Lewis flush with a left hook that staggers him. Bowe is unable to apply too much pressure with the Lion holding on and riding out the remainder of the round.

Between round Three and Six, both land some decent shots and have success with their jabs. When things get close, Bowe takes charge with his inside fighting, and when Lewis is able to keep things at a distance, he's firmly in control.

By Round Seven both are tiring from the hard blows landed and things are starting to get a little ragged, with some exciting exchanges occurring. Lewis uses his ramrod left jab to set up some destructive overhand rights that detonate on Bowe's chin. Even he is surprised that Big Daddy is still standing, and what's more, he's coming back with some great uppercuts and hooks on the inside.

Neither fighter is giving an inch, with no weakness or fear showing. They are both facing the other with valour. Punch for punch, blow for blow they are fighting in a rhythmic ballet of violence that is only found in boxing.

As Round Ten begins, the fight is dead even. Bowe comes in with his chin unprotected and Lewis lands a killer right, knocking him down. Big Daddy manages to get back on his feet and sees out the round.

Round Twelve is underway and the crowd is on their feet, applauding a very tough and evenly contested fight between two warriors. Both corners instruct their man to give it everything in the last round as the fight is too close to call.

Lewis and Bowe come to the centre of the ring, let their hands go and push to show the judges who wants it more. Both land some great shots and are still standing at the end of the round.

As the bell rings they embrace in a truly mesmerising display of guts, heart and will to win.

Verdict: Split decision win to Lewis.

FIGHT CARD NINE

Vitali Klitschko vs. Riddick Bowe

Sonny Liston vs. Wladimir Klitschko

Jack Dempsey vs. Muhammad Ali

Mike Tyson vs. Larry Holmes

George Foreman vs. Gene Tunney

Lennox Lewis vs. Jack Johnson

Jim Jeffries vs. Joe Frazier

Max Schmeling vs. Floyd Patterson

Co-main Event: Evander Holyfield vs. Ken Norton

Main Event: Rocky Marciano vs. Joe Louis

Vitali Klitschko vs. Riddick Bowe

Straight into Fight Card Nine, and what a banger of a fight to kick things off! In one corner you have Big Daddy Riddick Bowe, and staring him down in the other is Dr Ironfist, Vitali Klitschko. Two superheavyweights in one of the biggest fights on record, literally.

Both fighters match up well. Klitschko is slightly bigger by two inches in height and thirteen pounds in weight, but has a shorter reach by one inch. Klitschko has the slight edge in power and chin, but Bowe is faster, more skilled and has better ring IQ. A tough fight to call and convincing arguments can be made for both.

With Eddie Futch in his corner, Bowe comes into the fight knowing two things: first, that he is in for a tough fight and will likely endure some heavy punishment; and second, with his skill advantage and Klitschko's slow speed and lack of inside fighting, he will have to take it to his opponent and make him fight his fight.

Klitschko is also a very intelligent boxer and is aware of the disparity in speed and skill. He looks to pressure Bowe and land his massive right hand.

Bowe comes through some trying periods and even picks himself off the canvas, but his skill and speed advantage, combined with his similar size, make it difficult for the Ukrainian to establish a rhythm.

Verdict: Decision win to Bowe.

Sonny Liston vs. Wladimir Klitschko

Another fight that could go either way. You have Liston's power, reflexes and ramrod jab against Klitschko's equally impressive left jab, powerful overhand right and hand speed.

Even though Klitschko towers over Liston by five inches and approximately thirty pounds in weight, Liston's reach is longer by three inches, and this gives Klitschko some huge problems. He struggles to establish his own jab, and Liston hits just as hard, if not harder.

Dr Steelhammer's suspect chin struggles to hold up to the Big Bear's lethal jab and hooks, and once Liston lands a hard shot,

Klitschko starts to fight too defensively. It doesn't take Liston long to work over his foe and put him away.

Verdict: TKO win to Liston in Round Four.

Jack Dempsey vs. Muhammad Ali

Ali is even faster than Tunney and much bigger; Dempsey just doesn't have enough to even land a clean shot on Ali, let alone win some rounds or hurt him.

Verdict: Decision win to Ali.

Mike Tyson vs. Larry Holmes

Going by the fight they had in 1988, you could be forgiven for thinking that this won't be much of a contest. However you'd be very wrong. At the time, Holmes was already past his best and hadn't fought in two years. He took the fight merely for a payday.

The fight starts with a rampaging Tyson looking to end things early. Holmes is fully expecting the early onslaught and uses his height and longer reach to tie up Tyson and wrestle him around the ring.

The main issue for Holmes is that his focus on nullifying Tyson's attacks results in less focus on actually carrying out his own offensive shots. Holmes also doesn't possess the foot speed to actually avoid Kid Dynamite's strikes, and solely relies on tying him up.

With the Easton Assassin's lack of knockout power and unwillingness to engage, Iron Mike isn't too concerned and pushes the pace, landing some great ripping combinations both to the body and head.

During the middle rounds Holmes is starting to settle into the fight and establish his jab, throwing some of his own shots. Tyson is starting to tire slightly but given the relative ease of the fight to this point, still has plenty in the locker.

By Round Seven Holmes is pumping that jab in Tyson's face and starting to feel pretty confident at turning the fight around. However Tyson beautifully slips the jab and lands a clinical left hook, rocking Holmes. A flurry of quickfire punches send him crashing to the mat.

Holmes makes the count, however with glazed-over eyes the ref mercifully calls the fight off.

Verdict: TKO win to Tyson in Round Seven.

George Foreman vs. Gene Tunney

Tunney has the skills and speed to avoid Foreman for maybe a few rounds, however Foreman will catch up with him, and when he connects, it will be lights out. Tunney is too small and doesn't have the endurance of Ali to withstand such brutal punishment.

Verdict: KO win to Foreman in Round Four.

Lennox Lewis vs. Jack Johnson

I give Johnson about a snowball's chance in hell against Lewis. Lewis is just too big, too skilful and too powerful. He won't be afraid of anything coming from Johnson.

Verdict: TKO win to Lewis in Round Five.

Jim Jeffries vs. Joe Frazier

Quite a few one-sided fights on this card, and here's another. Jeffries doesn't have the skills or power to be able to keep off

Frazier, who holds pretty much all the advantages. A swift crushing left hook will put an end to this pretty early.

Verdict: KO win to Frazier in Round Three.

Max Schmeling vs. Floyd Patterson

Finally, we have a competitive and interesting fight that could go either way! On the one hand you have the blistering speed and combination punches of Floyd Patterson up against the beautiful counter-punching, ring IQ and big overhand right of Max Schmeling.

Looking at the tale of the tape, Patterson is two inches shorter, a few pounds lighter and has a reach disadvantage of six-and-a-half inches. He also doesn't hit as hard and definitely possesses the weaker chin, however this is balanced with sublime speed in both hands and feet, a great heart and good stamina.

A tough fight to pick and convincing arguments can be made for either fighter.

At the start of the fight Patterson comes out fast and lands some beautiful flashy shots, racking up some early rounds. However, once Schmeling settles into the fight, his punches start to have an effect on Patterson, who begins to slow. Schmeling starts landing some beautifully-timed overhand rights and the Gentleman of Boxing is in trouble.

By Round Eight the Black Uhlan of the Rhine (what a nickname!) is landing his right hand too frequently for Patterson's liking, and he finally hits the canvas and fails to make the count.

Verdict: KO win to Schmeling in Round Eight.

Co-main Event: Evander Holyfield vs. Ken Norton

Here is a circumstance where both fighters are known for their superb conditioning and heart. A tough, evenly-matched fight that will be a barnstormer.

In the red corner you have the chiselled Ken Norton, and in the blue corner the tough-as-nails Evander Holyfield. The top opponents they faced make up about thirty percent of the fighters in this book. Truly remarkable.

So how do both stack up?

To sum up, almost identically. They are the same height, with Holyfield being a few pounds heavier and Norton having two-and-a-half inches in reach. Head to head, Holyfield has the speed advantage both in hands and feet, better boxing skills, sturdier chin and superior ring IQ, while Norton is better defensively and hits slightly harder.

Both fighters come into the fight with fantastic conditioning, fully expecting a twelve-round slugfest. Neither hit hard enough to put the other away and this results in a great back-and-forth battle.

The contest starts with Norton coming out with his patented cross-armed defence and throwing his pawing jab. Holyfield is having real difficulties figuring out this unique style, all the while Norton is landing some crisp hard shots.

By Round Three Holyfield is starting to adapt his attacks and uses his speed to throw some good combinations. He is having particular success with starting his attacks with his hook/uppercut punch. It comes under the cross-armed defence and lands like a heat-seeking missile.

The middle rounds consist of some great action with Holyfield's huge heart on full display. The Real Deal just can't resist a tear up and loves to fight fire with fire.

Holyfield has also started to get closer to Norton while throwing shots to avoid dealing with the difficult guard at distance. Norton also has a tendency to throw looping punches that can be countered, and the faster more skilled Holyfield is more than happy to take advantage.

However Norton has been the busier fighter and pushed the pace the entire fight, something judges always favour.

By the twelfth round the crowd is on their feet, with the fight hanging in the balance. Some commentators are siding with Holyfield and some with Norton. In between rounds, both corners are screaming at their man to give it everything and leave it all in the ring.

The round starts with Norton still pushing the pace, coming forward, landing some stiff jabs and working over Holyfield's body. Those earlier body attacks from Norton have taken their toll on Holyfield, however he isn't showing any weaknesses to his opponent.

In the second minute of the round Holyfield lands a great one-two, pushing back Norton, and they both tie up.

The final thirty seconds and both are swinging away with no regard for defence. Norton lands a great right hand and Holyfield fires back with a jab and right hook. By the time the final bell rings both collapse into each other's arms and the crowd applauds a true spectacle.

Verdict: Split Decision win to Holyfield.

Main Event: Rocky Marciano vs. Joe Louis

I understand some may argue that, since this fight already happened, the result should stand. However Louis was way past his best and it would be unfair to use that version of him for this fight. So, to be clear, this is prime Louis from around 1938 against a prime Marciano from circa 1953.

Physically, Louis is taller by four inches, is ten pounds heavier and has a nine-inch reach advantage.

Both are hard hitters with great KO ratios of seventy-five and eighty-eight percent, respectively. One sparring partner of both fighters commented that one of Marciano's powerful punches was the equivalent of four of Louis'. Louis does however throw more combinations and doesn't load up on individual punches like the Rock does. Either way, I will give the slight power edge to Marciano, as well as chin, stamina and slightly more heart.

However Louis is by far the faster and better technical boxer and also has better ring IQ.

This will be a tough fight for both combatants. Marciano has declared that he will knock out Louis, while Louis simply replied that he does his talking with his fists.

With the announcer in the ring, he begins... "Ladies and gentlemen, it is now time for our main event of the evening. Hailing from Brockton, Massachusetts and weighing 184 pounds: the Brockton Bomber, Rocky Marciano! And his opponent from Chambers County, Alabama, weighing 194 pounds: the Brown Bomber, Joe Louis!"

The commentary team can't contain their excitement and are discussing the prospect of the two most dominant fighters from their respective decades going head-to-head.

Once the fighters have received their final instructions, they walk back to their corners and the bell rings. The fight is on.

Marciano comes powering ahead and lets some great body shots off while also throwing in some stiff hooks to the head. Louis ties the smaller man up and moves him onto the ropes. As they fight out of the clinch, Louis lands a great one-two and Marciano motions for his foe to come in and try that again.

The round ends with some good shots landed by both. Louis landed the cleaner punches, while Marciano really worked over Louis' body.

The second round gets underway and Marciano starts to crowd Louis and smother his work while landing some quickfire body attacks. Louis knows he can't take too much of this punishment and starts throwing some serious leather in return.

At the end of the second, both have won a round each.

The third round begins with more body shots from the Rock while the Brown Bomber ties off with some great accurate combinations, opening up a nasty cut above Marciano's left eye.

We are now into Round Four and while Louis is against the ropes, Marciano feints with the left and lands a pulverising right hand bang on the money. Louis is down and in serious trouble.

The ref motions Marciano to the neutral corner and begins his count. By eight Louis rises but is still pretty groggy. Marciano comes flying in and throwing rights, lefts and everything but the kitchen sink. He's looking to end this one, however Louis has the wherewithal to hold on and see out the round.

Throughout the build-up the fans have been split down the middle with their support. The class and dignity shown by both fighters has been exemplary, however nothing rouses a crowd more than an impending KO.

Round Five and Marciano is giving it his all, however Louis is too smart and avoids most shots to the head, enduring the heavy body blows. By the end of the round Louis has his legs back and has started putting some punches together. Nothing too devastating but letting Marciano and the judges know he's okay and ready for war.

In between rounds the Brown Bomber sits on his stool. A throbbing ache vibrates down his sides like a twisted torturer playing the accordion that is his ribs.

Round Six and, knowing he's behind, Louis comes out faster, throwing some beautifully strung together punches and working the cut above Marciano's eye. Louis is great at using his opponent's forward momentum against them and catches his foe coming in, scoring a quick flash knockdown. Marciano isn't too hurt and gets up at the count of four.

Round Seven and Louis is starting to judge the distance better and avoids Marciano crowding him too much. He is starting to land some hurtful shots that are taking their toll on the Brockton Bomber.

Rounds Eight and Nine have a similar theme, with Marciano coming forward and landing some hard body and head shots. But Louis' barrage of fast punches is too damaging and Marciano's face is awash with multiple cuts. His left eye has closed up from the relentless right hands that keep landing.

Round Ten and Marciano is fighting on instinct at this point; he just can't get out of the way of Louis' punches and towards the end of the round Louis lands a big right hand that knocks Marciano down for the second time.

Even though he's back up before ten, the ref has seen enough and waves off the fight.

Verdict: TKO win to Louis in Round Ten.

FIGHT CARD TEN

Sonny Liston vs. Joe Louis

Ken Norton vs. Jim Jeffries

Larry Holmes vs. Vitali Klitschko

Wladimir Klitschko vs. Jack Dempsey

Floyd Patterson vs. Evander Holyfield

Jack Johnson vs. Max Schmeling

Gene Tunney vs. Lennox Lewis

Triple Main Event: Riddick Bowe vs. George Foreman

Co-main Event: Joe Frazier vs. Rocky Marciano

Main Event: Muhammad Ali vs. Mike Tyson

The best fight card so far, with some epic fights. I struggled to decide on the top-billed showdowns so added a third main event. Two other stand-out fights that could have easily main evented on their own are Liston vs. Louis and Holmes vs. V. Klitschko.

So, without further ado, let's get the first fight underway.

Sonny Liston vs. Joe Louis

Here we have a tremendous opening fight, with the Brown Bomber Joe Louis squaring off against the Big Bear Sonny Liston. Both pack serious firepower in each fist and will be looking to take the other out as early as possible.

Louis is an inch taller but twenty pounds lighter and gives eight inches up in reach – quite the difference. Liston hits slightly harder, is more durable and is also the much stronger fighter, meaning Louis will struggle to push him around. However, Louis has the faster hands, better combination punching, heart and stamina. They are about even in terms of ring IQ, making this a real toss up of a fight.

The contest starts with both feeling each other out, fully aware of the power the other possesses. Liston's long hard jab gives Louis serious problems early on and provides Liston with some great opportunities to land some punishing blows with his right hand, building an early lead on the scorecards.

As the rounds progress, Louis' quality starts to show as he adjusts to Liston's attacks and forces the fight to the inside, where he lands some beautifully timed combinations and gives the Big Bear some food for thought.

By Round Six Liston is up three-two and is starting to apply the pressure. Louis, knowing he's behind, opens up more, looking to land some big shots. However, he leaves himself susceptible to the right uppercut and Liston lands a stunning shot, knocking Louis down. Louis makes the count, clears his head and rides out the round.

Round Seven begins and Liston's feeling pretty confident. He comes out looking for the finish and bombs start to fly. However, Louis has recovered and simply beats Liston to the punch, landing a blurring four-punch combo and down goes Liston.

The crowd is at fever pitch. Being behind on the cards and clearly outmuscled has made Louis ready to rumble. Liston is up at eight and needs a minute to clear his head, all the while Louis is opening up with left hooks, right hands and some hard jabs.

Round Eight begins and a sense of foreboding is in the air, with the feeling that one of these amazing warriors won't make it out of the round. The fighters walk to the centre and nod as a sign of mutual respect. Then the carnage begins.

Liston goes back to thudding out his jab and pushing Louis back. Louis is slipping the jab and coming into the inside with his flurries. Liston now fully aware of the danger of letting too many shots land constantly ties up Louis, leaning his heavier body on his opponent.

Even though Louis addressed his tendency to drop his left after throwing a jab post his first Schmeling fight, he still does it on occasion, and with his stationery head Liston finally sees the opening he's been searching for all night. He lands a poleaxing overhand right and Louis is down. And it's a heavy knockdown.

The commentators are worried for the Brown Bomber, but he rises as a true warrior does. However the ensuing onslaught causes the ref to step in and call the fight off. The audience are in awe at such a spectacle, having witnessed one of the best fights to mix power and technical skills.

Verdict: TKO win to Liston in Round Eight.

Ken Norton vs. Jim Jeffries

Norton is too awkward and has superior boxing skills compared to Jeffries. Norton has only lost to big punchers like Foreman or Shavers, or to fast and skilful fighters who kept the fight at range, such as Ali and Holmes. Jeffries will unfortunately not be able to outgun or outbox his opponent.

Verdict: Decision win to Norton.

Larry Holmes vs. Vitali Klitschko

Holmes will be wary of Klitschko's superior size and power advantage. He'll look to keep the fight at a distance, using his hard jab to box circles around his slower opponent.

The fight won't be the most exciting, and Holmes will have to come through some pretty precarious moments, but his speed and skill advantage can't be overlooked. Dr Ironfist just won't be able to cleanly catch the Easton Assassin enough times to sway the fight in his favour.

Verdict: Decision win to Holmes.

Wladimir Klitschko vs. Jack Dempsey

Dempsey is definitely fast enough to land on Klitschko, and he hits hard enough to absolutely brutalise his chin and send him into next week.

But the question is how W. Klitschko will approach this fight. From a sensible and tactical point of view, it is reasonable to expect a solid, risk-free game plan where Dr Steelhammer will rely on his jab and grab style and frustrate the much smaller man. I can see this fight being a tactical affair due to Klitschko's approach. He will continually fire out his jab and follow it up with his big overhand right.

Dempsey will try to slip the jab and come into the inside to land some quick and hard punches, but once on the inside Klitschko will just tie him up, lean on him and push him against the ropes. The size difference will be immense, like watching a middleweight against a superheavyweight.

And this won't be like the Willard fight. Klitschko is more skilled, hits just as hard as Dempsey and won't enter into any unnecessary exchanges.

Verdict: TKO win to W. Klitschko in Round Ten.

Floyd Patterson vs. Evander Holyfield

A very interesting fight, as Patterson is faster and will establish an early lead on the cards. Holyfield is just as active, but is the bigger man, has the strength advantage and the much tougher chin.

This fight goes the distance, with Holyfield scoring a couple of knockdowns along the way. But with Patterson's great heart he gets up each time and valiantly fights on.

From the halfway point the Real Deal takes over and uses his size and strength to wear down the slowing Patterson. However, with Holyfield's lack of real knockout power he struggles to finish the job.

A highly entertaining crowd-pleasing fight with some good back-and-forth action.

Verdict: Decision win to Holyfield.

Jack Johnson vs. Max Schmeling

Could this be Johnson's first win in the book?

Johnson will use his defensive prowess to nullify Schmeling's attacks and tie him up on the inside. Throw in some roughhousing from Johnson with intentional spoiling and Schmeling will find himself in uncharted waters.

A pretty slow, boring fight that will lack any real spark or action.

Verdict: Decision win to Johnson.

Gene Tunney vs. Lennox Lewis

As the saying goes, you can run but you can't hide. Tunney will try to avoid the bigger man but will eventually get clobbered into next week. Lewis is too big and strong.

Verdict: KO win to Lewis in Round Two.

Triple Main Event: Riddick Bowe vs. George Foreman

Forgive me for making three fights part of the main event, I just couldn't decide which one to downgrade.

In one corner you have Big Daddy Riddick Bowe and in the other Big George Foreman, both considered big, but who is the biggest? And who is the meanest?

Bowe is an inch taller, about seventeen pounds heavier and has two inches in reach. Normally the bigger fighter is the stronger, however Foreman isn't much smaller and is freakishly strong, so on balance I would say Foreman is the stronger fighter and certainly hits the harder of the two.

In terms of meanness, again Big George is one mean SOB in the ring.

This will easily be one of Bowe's biggest, toughest fights and you can expect him to come in tip-top shape with a perfect game plan devised by the late great Eddie Futch. The strategy will be straightforward: avoid exchanges and don't let Foreman land, especially while coming in with his walking left jab/hook punch. Get Foreman on the inside and then throw the uppercuts and hooks.

Foreman's strategy will be pretty simple as well: keep the fight at mid to long range (his preferred fighting distance) and land as many clean blows as possible to get the bigger man out of there quickly.

When Foreman made his comeback during the nineties he confirmed that he was only interested in fights with Holyfield and Tyson, being suspiciously quiet when it came to Bowe and Lewis. If this was old man Foreman in this fight, I think almost everyone would call Bowe the overwhelming favourite. Also, not wanting to get into the ring with such big, young heavyweights at the age of forty is understandable.

However, the version of Foreman we are focusing on is the one who pulverised a prime Frazier in two. Someone who will have no hesitation or fear in stepping up against Bowe.

Once the fight starts Bowe comes out tentatively, pawing his jab and keeping Foreman on the end of it. Every time they get up close, Bowe has some good success, landing some shots on the inside and tying up Foreman.

One thing Bowe is taken aback by is how much stronger his foe is, finding he is not able to move him around or push him back. Foreman is fully prepared for such tactics and doesn't let it affect him, displaying some great patience.

In Round Two Foreman lands a hurtful right hand that wobbles Bowe but is unable to finish him off before the round ends.

By Round Five Bowe is ahead in the fight, however has sustained some punishment and is feeling the effects of the hard shots. Foreman is a master of cutting off the ring and getting his opponent into firing range and as Bowe mistakenly steps to his left, a hard jab/hook lands flush, followed by a crushing right hand which sends him down for the count.

Bowe is up at seven but is feeling shaky. The ref takes a close look, let's the fight continue. Bowe's defence is just too leaky at points and Foreman continues to find the right shot at the right time.

Round Six starts and Bowe is still feeling the effects of the knockdown. Big George comes barrelling in, landing some tough shots, and Bowe is down again for the second time. He rises once again but his corner waves the fight off, knowing their fighter is out on his feet.

Verdict: TKO win to Foreman in Round Six.

Co-main Event: Joe Frazier vs. Rocky Marciano

The only undefeated fighter in this book against the winner of the *Fight of the Century* – this could easily be the main event and probably would have been under normal circumstances. Two great champions who fight with honour, courage, tremendous heart and crowd-pleasing and all-action styles.

Looking at the tale of the tape, Frazier is one inch taller, has six-and-a-half inches in reach and, most importantly, twenty pounds of muscle on the Rock. Frazier is also faster and the technically better boxer. Conversely, Marciano hits the harder of the two with both fists and has the better chin.

Both have lion-sized hearts and unlimited stamina, meaning this fight will be relentless from the first bell to the last.

During the build-up both fighters are extremely respectful of the other and conduct themselves with complete class. The public and pundits are torn, with strong cases made for both fighters coming out the victor.

Marciano always trains for each fight like it is his last, and Frazier comes in excellent shape, knowing full well he has a long and tough night ahead of him.

Round One and Marciano comes out to meet Frazier in the centre of the ring. They both start letting their fists fly. Frazier normally starts slow but with the insistence of his corner he comes out faster than usual.

Frazier lands a great left hook and Marciano shakes it off and follows it up with two body shots and a hard overhand right of his own. In the last thirty seconds Frazier dips to his left to set up his hook and walks straight into a huge right hand. He is down. The ref begins his count but Frazier isn't too hurt and is up at six. The round ends ten-eight to Marciano.

By Round Two Frazier has shaken off the cobwebs from the knockdown and makes a mental note to be wary of Marciano's big right. Again, both stand in the middle of the ring and trade shots, neither backing off. A tough round to score but Frazier was the busier fighter and landed the flashier shots.

By Round Three Smokin' Joe is starting to pick up the pace, but the Brockton Bomber isn't too concerned. He lands some great body shots and follows them up with a great uppercut, staggering Frazier back before they tie up.

This fight could have been fought in a telephone booth. By Round Four both fighters are like two bulls refusing to give an inch. The activity from both fighters is incredible, with each throwing over a hundred punches a round.

Frazier opens a deep cut over the Rock's right eye, and everyone is hoping the fight doesn't get called off. Marciano lands a great combination ending with a left hook of his own to nick the round.

Round Five and Marciano is surprised by Frazier's tenacity, as most fighters usually start slowing down around the middle of the fight. Marciano puts this to the back of his mind and starts throwing some bombs, teeing off with the right and landing a couple of beautifully timed shots.

Frazier pushes Marciano to the ropes and wails away to the body, following it up with a hard left hook that snaps Marciano's head back and breaks his nose. Tasting his own blood and being forced to breathe from his mouth enrages the Brockton Bomber.

By Round Six Frazier's ribs are feeling sore from the relentless body work of his opponent and Marciano's face is a bloody mess, with another smaller cut opening up above his left eye. Another tough round to score, with both having some great moments.

The commentators are starting to notice that Frazier's weight advantage is becoming a factor, with him pushing Marciano back more regularly than at the start of the fight.

Round Seven and with Frazier starting to use his weight advantage more, he is unsettling the Rock from sitting down on his punches, resulting in Marciano's shots not having the same sting. Frazier steps around to the left and lands a perfect left hook that sends Marciano down. Marciano is up at seven and nods to Frazier, beckoning him to come in. Frazier is more than happy to oblige, and they exchange hooks, then tie up.

Frazier's feeling pretty confident by Round Eight and comes out looking to end things, however Marciano still has plenty in the tank. The Rock feints with the left then lands a pulverising Suzie Q, sending Frazier crashing through the ring ropes. Everyone is on their feet and commenters are shouting, "Is the fight over?"

Marciano is in the neutral corner and the ref counts to twenty, giving Frazier more time to get back into the ring. Frazier is dazed but scrambles back in and the ref lets the fight continue after taking a very close look.

Marciano comes in throwing hooks, uppercuts and overhand rights. The sheer volume puts Frazier down again. The crowd collectively holds their breath as the count starts. Frazier gets up again at nine and the ref lets him continue.

The bell rings and Frazier staggers back to his corner. Twenty seconds longer and the fight could well have been over.

Frazier's corner do their best to settle the fighter who's still on shaky legs. They insist he doesn't come out recklessly for Round Nine and takes it a bit slow. He needs to find his legs and clear his head.

As the round starts, Marciano does his best to put Frazier away, but Frazier keeps tying him up and pushing him back up against the ropes. Towards the end of the round Frazier's head has cleared, and he starts throwing a few flurries, but doesn't land anything too spectacular.

The bell rings for Round Ten and Marciano comes out, continuing his relentless assault on Frazier's body, who is convinced a rib or two is broken. Frazier is starting to let his hands go and lands some well-timed left hooks, following them up with a nice overhand right. Both men are feeling the effects of such a brutal war.

Round Eleven and the knockdowns have titled the scorecards in Marciano's favour. Frazier is fully aware of this. The bell rings and he comes out swinging, landing some eye-catching left hooks and pushing Marciano back. The Rock fires back with his right and lands a great one-two. The round ends with Frazier landing another stunning left that rocks Marciano.

Entering the final round of a pulsating contest, the only thought that enters either fighter's mind is to land as many punches as possible.

The roar of the crowd is nothing but a faint echo. Instructions coming from the corners are not even registering, with time slowing for both. All they see are the small details that give away an opponent's next move. A slight quiver in the throat before a right cross is thrown. A subtle dip to the left to set up the left hook...

Everything is noticed by the boxers, and yet nothing outside the ring is of concern. Two courageous combatants entangled in the cruellest of dances.

The fight is too close to call. With Frazier sensing he needs to do something special; he doesn't let up. He steps to the left and lunges in with his hook, hitting Marciano right on the chin and sending his opponent down for the count.

Marciano manages to get to his feet but is on wobbly legs. Fans are shocked at the heart on display by both fighters.

Frazier comes in again but Marciano doesn't retreat, he simply does what he does best and throws the right hand, both trading hooks while up close. Marciano lands a right and Frazier hits with the left. This fight has been back and forth the entire time.

The bell rings and everyone is on their feet, clapping and cheering at having witnessed perhaps the greatest fight ever.

Verdict: Split decision win to Frazier.

Main Event: Muhammad Ali vs. Mike Tyson

This is the fight everyone has been waiting for. Perhaps the number one talked about fantasy matchup in boxing, with the two biggest stars in the history of the heavyweight division going head-to-head.

The build-up, the drama, the controversy … everything is on another level as two of the biggest personalities finally square off to see who will stand tall once the dust has settled.

Taking a step back, the fighters actually have quite a bit of shared history. While Tyson was in a youth detention centre, he actually met Ali after watching his movie *The Greatest*. Tyson described this moment in his life as the catalyst that got him into boxing.

A young Tyson also used to listen in to calls between his trainer Cus D'Amato and Ali, just to hear what they were talking about.

Once Tyson was the champ, both sat on the same couch during the Arsenio Hall show in 1989. When asked by the host who would have won, Ali said he would dance around but when hit he feigned being knocked out. Tyson simply said, "Ali is the greatest of all time."

After Tyson's loss to Douglas, Ali actually called a boxing journalist and claimed, "Are people now going to stop asking who would have won between us in our primes?"

Analysing the tale of the tape, Tyson is significantly shorter by five inches and has a smaller reach by seven inches, with their weight being about even.

Ali has never been the hardest hitter and Tyson clearly has the power advantage. Tyson relies on speed and explosiveness, however I can't see this being too much of an issue for Ali, who is even faster with both hands and feet. Ali also has the better chin, endurance, stamina, ring IQ and heart.

The key for Tyson will be to get Ali out of there early.

Once the fight is signed, Tyson comes into the press tour full of praise for his opponent, claiming this to be the honour of his career.

Ali, on the other hand, is in no such mood, proudly claiming to knock out the little bulldog (the name he coined Tyson with). During interviews, Ali brings along a toy bulldog and punches it in the face, constantly taunting and trying his best to humiliate Tyson at every turn.

Coming from the streets of Brooklyn there's only so much disrespect one can take, and Tyson finally snaps. Things almost come to blows when a pissed off Tyson shouts back that Ali "won't be pretty after he meets my fists", then scandalously proclaims that he will make Ali his "little bitch" in the ring.

Some observers rightfully claim this was a strategy by Ali to get into Tyson's head and play mind games.

Tickets for this super fight sell out in record time. Even though they are priced at a premium, fans have flocked from around the world to the famous Madison Square Garden. All box office records have been broken, with broadcasters clamouring to show the fight.

The boxing world is split, struggling to agree on who will win. One thing is for sure, by the time the main event starts the crowd will be at fever pitch.

With both fighters in the ring, Tyson stares ahead menacingly, trying to psyche out his opponent. Ali keeps trash talking, with the ref having to tell him to shut up while he gives the final instructions.

The fight starts with Tyson coming forward and throwing some hard body shots, following this up with some powerful hooks to the head. Ali is able to slip most of the shots and fires back with some fast combinations of his own. When they tie up Ali continues whispering in Tyson's ear, infuriating the Brooklyn native.

The first few rounds consist of Ali circling Tyson and throwing his fast jab, following it up with three-four punch combos – all straight shots – then gliding out of range. The Greatest's strategy is pretty clear; with his superior foot speed he is staying just out of range, with his shorter foe struggling to land his hardest shots.

By Round Five Tyson is clearly behind and is enraged. He comes flying out of his corner and throws some scary blows.

Ali stays a little too long in the pocket and Tyson finally lands a flush left hook, which sends Muhammed crashing into the ropes. He manages to stay upright, grabbing hold of the marauding Tyson and whispering in his ear, "Is that all you got, sucka?"

Tyson keeps letting his fists fly, but Ali is too experienced and avoids most of the attacks. At best a glancing blow or two lands, reminding Ali of the power his rival possesses.

As the fight progresses Ali has an answer for all of Tyson's attacks. While they tie up Ali mercilessly taunts him, leans on him and pushes his head down, sapping Tyson of much needed energy.

By Round Ten Tyson is pretty deflated. His left eye has swollen closed and a gash above his right eye has opened up, causing blood to pour into his eye.

Tyson's corner is yelling at him to give everything he has. Even though it has been a tough fight, Ali is still dancing around and firing off attacks like it's the first round.

Iron Mike is now getting desperate. Knowing he's behind on the cards, his punches are becoming wilder, something Ali is happy to take advantage of as he lands a string of shots and knocks Kid Dynamite down for the first time in the fight.

Tyson makes the count. The ref takes a very close look but lets the fight continue.

Ali comes in and lands another great flurry. The commentators are questioning how Tyson is staying up. Another overhand right from Ali sends Tyson stumbling to the ropes and the ref finally steps in, waving the fight off.

The audience are stunned, having witnessed a masterful performance by the Greatest who came into the fight with the perfect game plan and executed it flawlessly.

Verdict: TKO win to Ali in Round Ten.

Summary: Fight Cards Six to Ten

We are now over halfway through with ten fight cards complete and in the record books. It's been an incredible run of fights that have included brutal KOs, spectacular wins and masterclass displays of boxing.

Only two fighters – Lennox Lewis and Muhammad Ali – are undefeated, and we can expect a colossal contest between the two during the upcoming fight cards.

Mike Tyson lost his undefeated streak in the last five fights, succumbing to Ali and Foreman in two brutal battles. Holmes has dropped out of the top five, being replaced by Liston who went from three-two to seven-three with big wins over Foreman, Dempsey, W. Klitschko and Louis.

All fighters have now got their first win, with the standout fighter being Joe Frazier, who strung together five straight wins over Bowe, Johnson, Louis, Jeffries and Marciano.

Some of the best fights included:

- Joe Louis vs. Sonny Liston
- Joe Frazier vs. Riddick Bowe
- Sonny Liston vs. George Foreman
- Mike Tyson vs. George Foreman
- Rocky Marciano vs. Joe Frazier (Out of a hundred fights so far, this was easily the most exciting and epic – a real fight for the ages.)

Current League Standings After Ten Fight Cards

		Wins	Losses	Draws	Points
1	Lennox Lewis	10			30
2	Muhammad Ali	10			30
3	George Foreman	8	2		24
4	Mike Tyson	8	2		24
5	Sonny Liston	7	3		21
6	Evander Holyfield	6	4		18
7	Joe Frazier	6	4		18
8	Joe Louis	6	4		18
9	Larry Holmes	6	4		18
10	Wladimir Klitschko	6	4		18
11	Riddick Bowe	5	5		15
12	Vitali Klitschko	5	5		15
13	Ken Norton	4	6		12
14	Gene Tunney	3	7		9
15	Jack Dempsey	3	7		9
16	Max Schmeling	2	8		6
17	Rocky Marciano	2	8		6
18	Floyd Patterson	1	9		3
19	Jack Johnson	1	9		3
20	Jim Jeffries	1	9		3

Let's see how the next five cards shape up. At the moment both Lewis and Ali are dominating, but with some hard fights ahead, will they be able to maintain their perfect records?

FIGHT CARD ELEVEN

Riddick Bowe vs. Jack Dempsey

Muhammad Ali vs. Sonny Liston

Rocky Marciano vs. Jim Jeffries

Gene Tunney vs. Mike Tyson

Jack Johnson vs. Vitali Klitschko

Floyd Patterson vs. George Foreman

Ken Norton vs. Lennox Lewis

Joe Frazier vs. Max Schmeling

Co-main Event: Larry Holmes vs. Wladimir Klitschko

Main Event: Joe Louis vs. Evander Holyfield

Riddick Bowe vs. Jack Dempsey

W hen I approached this fight I initially felt Bowe would be too big and too strong for Dempsey, resulting in a straightforward win. However after looking into things I realised that Dempsey is a similar size to Holyfield but hits a lot harder and is way more aggressive.

Bowe is four inches taller, has seven inches in reach and about forty-seven pounds of muscle on his smaller foe. On balance I would say Dempsey hits harder (though not by much), is a little faster and has better stamina. Where Bowe has the edge is ring IQ and pure boxing skills, especially with his inside fighting and size.

So how will the fight play out?

Once the bell sounds, Dempsey comes out fast, landing some great shots and putting the pressure on early. Bowe rides out the onslaught and takes over with his superior boxing skills, landing some telling uppercuts and hooks while on the inside.

The Manassa Mauler loves getting up close and landing his slashing punches, but Bowe's too good to allow such a devastating finisher too many openings and controls the pace by constantly tying up Dempsey and frustrating him.

Big Daddy Bowe isn't the slow and lumbering Willard, and Dempsey has huge problems with the skill and size disparity between the two. Once Big Daddy settles into the fight, he starts wearing down the smaller man and eventually finishes him off with a powerful two-punch combination.

Verdict: TKO win to Bowe in Round Six.

Muhammad Ali vs. Sonny Liston

I will be ignoring the second fight that had the infamous "phantom punch" and the clear controversy surrounding it. All we need to look at is the first bout, which had its own fair share of controversy, but still provided us with a clear winner.

Ali is simply too fast for Liston. If they fought a hundred times Ali would win over ninety of them, maybe more.

Verdict: TKO win to Ali in Round Six.

Rocky Marciano vs. Jim Jeffries

Here we have an interesting and extremely competitive fight between the only two boxers in this book to retire undefeated as the heavyweight champion (Jeffries did come out of retirement in a losing effort to Johnson).

Neither fighter is the most technical, but makes up for this with supreme conditioning, heart and work rate. Jeffries is the bigger fighter at six feet one-and-a-half inches, has the longer reach by nine-and-a-half inches and about forty-one pounds on the Rock in weight.

Marciano has the advantage in power, chin and heart, with Jeffries being faster, naturally bigger and possessing slightly more ring IQ. Both have great stamina and could easily fight at a blistering pace for fifteen rounds.

Once the bell goes it is like witnessing two bulls charging ahead. Neither fighter knows how to take a backwards step and both show no signs of weakness.

Jeffries takes the early lead, landing some brilliant punches on Marciano's chin. Marciano starts slow and works his way into the fight, constantly pushing Jeffries back to the ropes and working over his body, looking for some ferocious head shots.

By Round Five Jeffries has opened up cuts above both of Marciano's eyes and blood is streaming down his face. This just drives the Rock further, and he takes full advantage of Jeffries' poor defence and tendency to keep his left hand outstretched and right hand by his side, telegraphing too many of his shots. This allows Marciano to get on the inside and land some bruising hooks.

In Round Five a well-timed feint from the Rock gives him the perfect opening and he lands the overhand right, knocking Jeffries down and shattering his nose in the process. Jeffries gets to his feet and isn't too concerned with his broken nose, having experienced three different nose breaks already in his career.

Jeffries' reliance on clinching and wrestling is proving to be pretty ineffective as Marciano is an expert in the clinch, and fighting in the pocket is his favoured position.

After a gruelling ten rounds Jeffries is sporting three broken ribs, a broken nose, several cuts and a closed-up eye, but he's still got enough in the tank to see out the last two rounds.

Verdict: Decision win to Marciano.

Gene Tunney vs. Mike Tyson

On the face of it, Tunney could do to Tyson what he accomplished against Dempsey – frustrate Tyson by fighting on the back foot while staying out of range. However, considering things further, Tunney won't be fighting a rusty and semi-retired Jack Dempsey; he will be in there with a prime, sharp and active Iron Mike Tyson.

Kid Dynamite also carries thirty pounds of muscle on the Fighting Marine and throws sublime combinations with both hands. Tunney will have no answer for such varied and ferocious attacks, especially with his tendency to fight with a low guard and to lean back to avoid punches.

Verdict: KO win to Tyson in Round Four.

Jack Johnson vs. Vitali Klitschko

Johnson is the more skilled fighter, especially in terms of defence, however his lack of power and the massive size difference between the two will make for an easy night's work for Dr Ironfist.

Verdict: TKO win to V. Klitschko in Round Two.

Floyd Patterson vs. George Foreman

If Liston could brutalise Patterson, can you imagine what a prime George Foreman could do? A highlight reel KO and early night for Big George.

Verdict: KO win to Foreman in Round One.

Ken Norton vs. Lennox Lewis

Norton will make it a little tricky for the Lion with his awkward cross guard defence and great stamina, however once Lewis makes a couple of adjustments, his hard jab and powerful overhand right will make light work of Norton.

Verdict: TKO win to Lewis in Round Four.

Joe Frazier vs. Max Schmeling

It's been a pretty straightforward card so far, and this fight is no exception. Schmeling won't know how to handle Frazier's bobbing and weaving. The brutal left hooks will find their mark too often for Schmeling's liking. He will gallantly fight on and land some solid right hands, but nothing to worry Smokin' Joe, who will find the finishing punch fairly early on.

Verdict: TKO win to Frazier in Round Five.

Co-main Event: Larry Holmes vs. Wladimir Klitschko

This fight will be labelled the "Battle of the Jabs", as both are great fighters known for their excellent left jabs. This will be a competitive and technically fantastic boxing match between two of the longest reigning champions in history at seven and ten years, respectively. A fight for the boxing purists.

Looking at the tale of the tape, Holmes is the shorter man by three inches and weighs about twenty-eight pounds less. They both have an eighty-one inch reach.

Klitschko is clearly the harder puncher with a concussive overhand right hand, while Holmes possesses the stronger chin. Both have about the same speed and they are about even in terms of heart, stamina and ring IQ. A very well-balanced fight.

During the build-up Holmes tries to get under his opponent's skin, calling him a "poor man's Gerry Cooney", while Klitschko simply retorts that Holmes' best win was against an old Muhammad Ali.

Once the fight starts both come out tentatively, feeling out their opponent and finding their range. Holmes lands a few snappy-looking jabs in the first couple of rounds and follows them up with the right, but Klitschko is able to see them coming, taking the sting out of them.

Holmes starts Round Three with his chin slightly out and Klitschko lands a great one-two, ending with a fierce right that sends Holmes back. The Easton Assassin is able to ride out the rest of the round but makes a mental note not to take too many of those flush.

Dr Steelhammer is starting to frustrate Holmes with his constant clinching when up close and keeps leaning his weight on the smaller fighter. During the middle rounds Klitschko fully settles into the fight and uses his superior size to control the distance and pace.

Holmes relies on parrying too many shots, which is an attempt to make up for his lack of head movement, but Klitschko's fast hands are landing more than they should be. Holmes is starting to feel the fight is getting away from him and is down on all three cards by the end of Round Nine.

In Round Ten Holmes comes out looking to land some big shots and swing the fight in his favour. He starts the round fast, landing some great combinations, but just doesn't have the firepower to unsettle Klitschko.

Holmes lingers on the ropes a little too long and Klitschko whips out the right, connecting smack bang on Holmes' jaw. He's down.

The ref is at seven... eight... nine...

The Easton Assassin rises but is still a little shaky. Dr Steelhammer doesn't come in for the kill, opting to stick to jabbing and wearing down his opponent. Both combatants make it to the end of the twelfth and embrace in a sign of mutual respect.

Verdict: Decision win to W. Klitschko.

Main Event: Joe Louis vs. Evander Holyfield

What a spectacle of a fight we have here. The longest-reigning heavyweight champion in history going head to head with the only four-time world champion in the heavyweight division.

In terms of height and reach, both are about the same, with Holyfield having a weight advantage of twenty-three pounds. Louis is by far the harder puncher and has the stamina advantage, with Holyfield having the sturdier chin and slightly higher ring IQ.

There isn't much between these two amazing fighters. Both will come in the best shape of their careers, fully anticipating a long and tough fight.

Louis comes out throwing his snapping jab and following it up with some sharp, fast combinations. Holyfield shrugs them off and comes steaming forward, trying to turn the fight into an all-out war. Round One sets the tone for the entire fight, with Holyfield trying to establish his jab but being beaten to the punch, then throwing some hooks of his own to retaliate.

The first few rounds go in favour of Louis, with the judges impressed with his flashy combinations and higher work rate.

By Round Five Holyfield has made some adjustments in sticking to his boxing and counters. With Louis slowing, the Real Deal starts to control the pace and lands some clean shots. Holyfield is also using his head quite a bit when up close and the Brown Bomber is starting to get annoyed with the constant butting, especially since a cut has opened up above his left eye.

By the end of Round Eight Louis is ahead, five rounds to three, but Holyfield is still coming on strong and pushing the pace.

Louis' corner instruct him to get back to pumping out the jab first, then following it up with his right hook, which he was having good success with early on. Louis comes out for the ninth and goes back to basics, pawing out his jab and following it up with another two-three punches. This is a weapon that is winning him the fight, as Holyfield is clearly having problems with countering it.

Holyfield is also struggling to roll with the punches and take the sting out of them. Normally he is a master of such a technique, however Louis' sharp and accurate shots are finding their target more often than not.

The bell sounds for the start of the final round and the crowd applaud in appreciation. Knowing he's behind, Holyfield comes out swinging, not leaving anything to chance. Louis is also pushing through the pain barrier and fighting on, hitting back with hooks and crosses of his own.

Holyfield just doesn't have the power to truly worry Louis and as they stand centre of the ring trading punch for punch, the whole arena is on their feet. The final bell sounds and we go to the judges.

Verdict: Decision win to Louis.

FIGHT CARD TWELVE

Sonny Liston vs. Larry Holmes

Wladimir Klitschko vs. Gene Tunney

Jack Dempsey vs. Jack Johnson

Mike Tyson vs. Floyd Patterson

Vitali Klitschko vs. Ken Norton

Max Schmeling vs. Rocky Marciano

George Foreman vs. Joe Frazier

Evander Holyfield vs. Jim Jeffries

Co-main Event: Muhammad Ali vs. Riddick Bowe

Main Event: Lennox Lewis vs. Joe Louis

Sonny Liston vs. Larry Holmes

Our twelfth fight card starts with a difficult fight to pick a winner for. You have the Easton Assassin Larry Holmes squaring off against the Big Bear Sonny Liston.

One of the strongest weapons for both fighters is their jabs. Holmes fires out his like a whip, fast and accurate, whereas Liston's jab is like a piston, carrying enough power to knock fighters down and completely unsettle them.

Liston has problems with movers, as witnessed in the Ali fights, while Holmes struggles with hard hitters, having come off the canvas himself against Shavers and Snipes. Holmes will easily be the most complete and technical fighter Liston has ever faced, and Liston will be one of the hardest hitters and ferocious finishers Holmes has had the honour of sharing a ring with.

Holmes is slightly taller by two inches, with Liston having the longer reach by three. Both weigh exactly the same. Liston has the power and chin advantage while Holmes is the better boxer, faster with both hands and feet and has more heart, stamina and ring IQ. Liston's boxing skills, while not up to par with Holmes', are still very good. With his hard punches and long reach, he will give Holmes some big issues.

Once the fight starts Liston comes forward, looking to establish his jab, but Holmes is just a little too quick moving in and out of position, lashing his own jab out like a whip.

Whenever they get up close Holmes cleverly ties up Liston but is surprised at the raw strength of the Big Bear. While up close Liston fires some nice hooks and lands a couple of glancing blows before Holmes moves out of position.

By Round Four Holmes is leading on the cards but isn't getting too ahead of himself, knowing the power his opponent possesses.

Liston has picked up on Holmes occasionally dropping his right and once in position waits for his moment of opportunity like a coiled cobra waiting to pounce. Holmes' right doesn't snap back into position and Liston strikes, landing a rock hard left hook that sends Holmes back into the corner. The Big Bear follows this up with a crushing overhand right, snapping Holmes' head back.

The Easton Assassin is face-down on the canvas.

The ref is at five and Holmes is using the ropes to get up. The ref signals for him to walk to him, which he manages (barely), and the fight goes on.

On cue Liston comes in, looking to land the finishing blow. But surprisingly he isn't throwing the kitchen sink at his hurt foe. Liston is staying composed and looking for the perfect shot to take out his opponent.

Holmes manages to survive the round and staggers back to his corner. During the interval Holmes is trying to stay calm and not panic. His corner is pleading with him to take the round off and get his legs back.

The fifth round clearly goes to Liston, who doesn't rush in but takes his time in controlling the pace with his hard jab, working over Holmes.

By Round Six Holmes is feeling back to his usual self and goes back to boxing, keeping things simple with a jab, right cross and then moving out of range.

By Round Ten the fight is on a knife edge with both fighters having great successes. Holmes is controlling the rounds for the most part, but every now and then Liston lands a hard shot and Holmes has to hold while getting roughed up on the inside.

Round Eleven begins and Liston is again looking to land one big right. He manages to get his tiring foe in position on the ropes and BOOM! The big right connects on Holmes' left cheek and he's down for the count. He manages to get to his feet, but the shot has completely disorientated him.

The ref mercilessly calls off the fight.

Verdict: TKO win to Liston in Round Eleven.

Wladimir Klitschko vs. Gene Tunney

While being the faster fighter, Tunney just doesn't have the power or size to keep Klitschko off him. This will end with a brutal right from Dr Steelhammer.

Verdict: KO win to W. Klitschko in Round Four.

Jack Dempsey vs. Jack Johnson

An aggressive come-forward puncher versus a defensive counter-punching boxer. A great mix that will provide an entertaining fight while it lasts.

Johnson starts well, landing some good counters and tying up Dempsey when up close. While Johnson has his opponent in the clinch, he fires some hard uppercuts that hit the target while Dempsey is crouching.

However, Johnson mistimes an uppercut and with Dempsey's now free left he unloads a cracking hook that hits Johnson square on the chin. A further three-four punch combination sends Johnson down for the count.

The Galveston Giant is back on his feet but for the following two rounds is fighting on the back foot. With his low punch output and lack of power the Manassa Mauler is just gaining in confidence.

By Round Seven Dempsey has worked over his opponents face and body, with Johnson sporting a closed left eye and some heavily bruised ribs. Dempsey comes on strong and manages to land some crisp shots that put his foe back down to the canvas. This time the ref has seen enough and waves the fight off.

Verdict: TKO win to Dempsey in Round Seven.

Mike Tyson vs. Floyd Patterson

Patterson has had two tough back-to-back fights going against Tyson and Foreman.

Cus D'Amato trained both fighters with a similar peek-a-boo style, and the general consensus is that Tyson is the better practitioner of said technique. Now, assuming Cus will stay neutral and let the fighters settle their differences in the ring, the question is whether Patterson is fast enough to avoid Tyson's attacks.

The short answer is, most likely, no. Liston brutalised Patterson and he isn't as fast as a prime Iron Mike. Tyson will definitely land on Patterson's chin and once that happens the fight can only go one way.

Verdict: KO win to Tyson in Round Two.

Vitali Klitschko vs. Ken Norton

This is a fight of opposites. You have the sturdiest chin in this book with Klitschko having never been knocked down, against Norton who is known to have a pretty weak chin.

Norton is the better boxer, but he doesn't hit hard enough to worry Dr Ironfist, who will also be the much bigger fighter. Once Klitschko gets through Norton's awkward defence, a few hard shots will send him down and out.

Verdict: TKO win to V. Klitschko in Round Four.

Max Schmeling vs. Rocky Marciano

Schmeling will pose some problems for Marciano, especially with his hard overhand right, however Marciano's relentless work rate and granite chin will slowly wear down Schmeling, who just won't have the firepower to take out the Rock early. He will have to endure a long, tough night of hard body shots and bludgeoning punches to the head.

Verdict: TKO win to Marciano in Round Eleven.

George Foreman vs. Joe Frazier

This fight happened twice: once in Jamaica 1973, where Foreman brutally knocked out Frazier, and again in 1976 when Frazier was able to last until the fifth round but suffered the same fate.

Smokin' Joe's swarmer style is tailor-made for Big George and if they fought ten times, you'd expect Foreman to win every one.

Verdict: TKO win to Foreman in Round Two.

Evander Holyfield vs. Jim Jeffries

Holyfield is just too fast and technical for Jeffries and his solid chin will have no trouble absorbing any shots that come his way, even Jeffries' best.

Verdict: Decision win to Holyfield.

Co-main Event: Muhammad Ali vs. Riddick Bowe

In 1992, perhaps the most disgraceful event in heavyweight championship boxing occurred. Riddick Bowe, acting on instructions from his manager Rock Newman, called a press conference and literally threw the WBC belt into the trash, in the process avoiding a fight with Lennox Lewis, his mandatory challenger.

In later years Bowe showed genuine regret and remorse over his actions, however in this alternative universe he has just pissed off one of the most old-school fighters there is.

Muhammad Ali was watching the press conference and was shocked at the blatant disrespect towards the sport, the WBC and fellow boxers. Ali is pissed and is coming for Bowe.

Once the fight is signed, Rock Newman makes his presence known, telling everyone who cares to listen that Ali is too small and just doesn't hit hard enough to trouble Bowe. Ali fires back, calling Bowe "Big Baby" for hiding behind Newman and letting him pull all the strings.

Physically, Bowe has the advantage, being two inches taller, twenty pounds heavier and with three extra inches in reach. Ali is by far the faster of the two, with more heart, stamina and ring IQ. Where Bowe excels is with having more power and being a bigger and better inside fighter.

On paper, the fight is pretty close, but how would things play out?

The fight starts with Bowe coming forward and controlling the centre of the ring. But this is where Ali wants him. Ali is more than happy to dance around the outside, just staying out of range while coming in with his fast combinations, then quickly moving out of position.

Bowe is struggling to pin down his opponent, noticing how much faster his feet and movements are. The blurring combinations are hard to read and are really jarring for Bowe. Bowe is struggling to get his timing down every time he throws the jab, Ali comes over the top with a lightning-fast right cross-counter, then ties him up.

A perfect strategy to avoid Bowe's inside game.

By Round Five Bowe has lost every round and is starting to feel frustrated at being unable to use his size or shots on the inside. He starts letting his hands go a little too wildly for his corner's liking.

Bowe manages to land a couple of good shots on Ali's chin, but his opponent absorbs the punishment and keeps on moving. Whenever they tie up, Bowe uses his bulk to push Ali around and tire him out.

During the championship rounds Ali is starting to slow ever so slightly and Bowe comes on strong, landing some flush uppercuts on the inside followed by some powerful hooks.

Round Twelve begins with Ali coming out wanting to close the show strong. He fires out his jab and follows it up with a blistering three-punch combination, which stuns Bowe. He shakes it off and throws some hard shots of his own, landing a cracking right hook on Ali's chin, which results in the Greatest covering up and initiating a clinch.

By the last thirty seconds Ali has cleared his head and is teeing off on Big Daddy, landing a hard jab, then a right followed by a swift left hook and another right. The audience are in awe at the speed and accuracy of such beautiful boxing so late on in the fight.

Both make it to the end of the fight and show respect to the other for a tough battle.

Verdict: Decision win to Ali.

Main Event: Lennox Lewis vs. Joe Louis

Here is a fight that, when broken down, is actually a lot closer than expected. You have the Lion Lennox Lewis going toe to toe with the Brown Bomber Joe Louis. USA versus the UK.

Lewis is three inches taller and has about fifty pounds of weight and eight inches in reach on Louis. They are both powerful punchers and could easily KO the other. Louis is faster with his hands, but not necessarily with his feet. They are even on chin and heart, with Louis having the better stamina and Lewis the better ring IQ. A finely balanced pugilistic affair.

Both fighters are known for their tremendous power and finishing ability. Louis brings an excellent seventy-five percent KO ratio compared to seventy-two percent for Lewis, so one thing is for certain, this isn't going the distance.

The build-up to the fight is amicable and full of class. Each fighter has the utmost respect for the other and is not overlooking the task ahead of them. During the press conference Lewis reiterates that he intends to make it a chess match, while Louis just said he'll be putting Lewis to sleep.

Lewis is fully aware of Louis' strengths and with the help of Emanuel Steward has devised the perfect game plan, relying on his size and skill to control the pace and taking minimal risks.

Louis' strategy is quite different. He aims to put it on his foe early and to try to knock him out. Entering into a long technical fight against a bigger and possibly more skilled opponent isn't a good idea.

The Brown Bomber is a perfect name because as soon as the first bell rings, he comes rushing over, throwing some deadly bombs. Lewis is caught off guard at such a fast start and tries to move out of position, but Louis is on him like white on rice, throwing a brutal three-punch combination which staggers the Brit. Louis follows it up with a vicious right hand and Lewis is down.

The crowd is on their feet. Could we see an early finish?

Lewis gets up and when Louis comes charging in he ties him up and starts out-muscling him. Louis is trying his best to land another clean shot, sensing it would end the fight, but Lewis is too canny and keeps smothering Louis' work and engaging in clinches. Lewis manages to get to the bell and is now fully alert to the danger his adversary brings.

Round Two and Louis again comes out throwing hard jabs and following them up with some nice three-punch combinations.

After the midpoint of the round Lewis has shaken off the cobwebs and wants to let Louis know he's in for a fight. Lewis has made a mental note that each time Louis throws some shots his slow feet don't get him out of range fast enough, so the Lion sees his opening. A brutal overhand right almost takes Louis' head off.

Louis crumples to the floor and the commentators indicate that the fight could be over. However, the Brown Bomber is as tough as they come, managing to get to his feet and ride out the round, not throwing too many punches.

On Louis' way back to his corner he can be heard saying that was the hardest punch he's ever been hit with.

With both fighters knowing that one mistake can end the fight, they both approach things a little more cautiously. Some really good boxing is on display here, with both fighters going back to using their great jabs and working their way in before throwing some hard shots.

Lewis' longer reach and ramrod jab is allowing him to control the pace and the next few rounds are a bit quiet, with neither fighter willing to commit too much to their power shots.

The pace is starting to have an effect on Lewis, who by Round Eight is starting to tire. However he is up on the cards five-three, with both scoring a knockdown apiece. Lewis is also using his weight advantage, constantly pushing Louis' head down and leaning on him, employing some roughhouse and dirty boxing tactics to keep up the pressure.

Round Nine begins and Louis comes in fast. Knowing he's behind on the cards, he tries to force the action. Lewis is fully aware of this and manages to keep Louis on the end of his jab, following it up with hard rights.

Towards the end of the round Lewis has Louis tied up and manages to free his right hand, then out of nowhere Lewis puts everything into a vicious uppercut which launches Louis off his feet. Louis is down and the ref starts the count, but waves it off at five. Louis is in no condition to continue.

Verdict: KO win to Lewis in Round Nine.

FIGHT CARD THIRTEEN

Rocky Marciano vs. George Foreman

Gene Tunney vs. Larry Holmes

Jack Johnson vs. Muhammad Ali

Floyd Patterson vs. Wladimir Klitschko

Ken Norton vs. Jack Dempsey

Jim Jeffries vs. Lennox Lewis

Evander Holyfield vs. Max Schmeling

Joe Louis vs. Vitali Klitschko

Co-main Event: Riddick Bowe vs. Sonny Liston

Main Event: Joe Frazier vs. Mike Tyson

Rocky Marciano vs. George Foreman

Unlucky for some, Fight Card Thirteen gets underway.

The opening bout is titled "A Force of Nature": you have Foreman and Marciano coming in with eighty-four and eighty-eight percent knockout ratios, respectively. Both have sturdy chins and an all-out attack style, never taking a backwards step. This will be the heavyweight equivalent of Naz-Kelley.

Physically, Foreman has all the advantages; he is taller by six inches, heavier by thirty pounds and has a massive twelve-inch reach advantage. Both are extremely strong, however again

Foreman is definitely the stronger fighter and has the more impressive KOs to his name – namely Frazier, Norton and Moorer.

If this were a video game, both would have the power bar turned to max with how hard they hit. In terms of chin and speed, both are about even, though Marciano has more heart and stamina. For boxing IQ, Foreman has the edge, as well as being the better boxer, but he always prefers to just blast out his opponents as fast as possible.

Round One begins with both coming to the centre and trading shot for shot. Foreman is an expert at cutting off the ring, a result of thousands of drills during training with Archie Moore. However this just goes out the window as Marciano comes straight for him.

The Rock throws a huge right hand which connects, and Big George is down in the first thirty seconds. He manages to rise, shakes his head and beckons his foe in. Marciano complies and walks straight into a huge right and is down himself.

The crowd is blown away, unable to process everything that is happening.

Marciano is up and both clinch, Marciano is having no success with Foreman on the inside as he's just too big and strong.

Towards the end of the round Foreman times a perfect walking left hook, which stuns the Brockton Bomber, then a vicious right puts the Rock down again. Once more he gets up, but the round ends.

The commentary team are beside themselves at having witnessed one of the most exciting rounds in boxing history.

Round Two begins, and Marciano comes out again with his chin in the air. Foreman connects with another hard overhand right which sends him down once more. He makes the count, but again

Foreman is too strong a finisher, gunning ahead and landing another hard left, sending Marciano down again. Somehow Marciano rises and makes it to the end of the round, but it's not looking promising.

Foreman is simply too big, too strong and hits way too hard for Marciano's liking. But being the warrior that the Rock Is, he comes out for the third, determined to turn the fight around. However, Foreman is fully alert to Marciano's main weapon (his right hand) and moves to his left while unloading hard shots of his own.

Marciano's face is busted open with cuts above both eyes and visible bruising down the left side. Nonetheless, he keeps coming forward, displaying a great warrior mentality.

Towards the end of Round Three Foreman lands another crushing right, and Marciano is down and struggling. The ref starts his count but can't let the fight continue, waving off the contest.

Verdict: TKO win to Foreman in Round Three.

Gene Tunney vs. Larry Holmes

This will be a fight geared towards the boxing purists. Both are skilful with good movement, however Holmes' size and great jab will be too much for Tunney. A very technical and unexciting fight for the most part.

Verdict: Decision win to Holmes.

Jack Johnson vs. Muhammad Ali

Johnson will have no answer to the faster, busier and bigger fighter. A very one-sided contest will end in whatever round Ali predicts before the fight.

Verdict: TKO win to Ali in Round Six.

Floyd Patterson vs. Wladimir Klitschko

Once Klitschko's right hand lands, it will be lights out for the Rabbit. And unfortunately for Patterson, it will happen pretty early.

Verdict: KO win to W. Klitschko in Round Three.

Ken Norton vs. Jack Dempsey

Norton was stopped by big punchers like Foreman and Shavers, and even though Dempsey doesn't hit quite as hard as them, he can definitely crack. Combined with his speed and reflexes, it will be all over for Norton from the first bell.

Verdict: KO win to Dempsey in Round Three.

Jim Jeffries vs. Lennox Lewis

Jeffries' defence just won't hold up against the boxing skills of Lewis. One hard overhand right will end things pretty swiftly for the Lion.

Verdict: KO win to Lewis in Round Two.

Evander Holyfield vs. Max Schmeling

Holyfield doesn't hit hard enough to be able to stop Schmeling, who is very durable, but he does possess sublime boxing skills and heart that will enable him to control the entire fight. Likewise, Schmeling can't hit hard enough to really worry the Real Deal.

Verdict: Decision win to Holyfield.

Joe Louis vs. Vitali Klitschko

This fight is a difficult one to judge. Both fighters have great strengths and strong arguments can be made for either winning.

The general consensus from my online research is a Klitschko win, but a large portion of fans have put forward convincing cases for Louis. You can point to how Louis handled the similarly-sized Primo Carnea, however Klitschko's much stronger chin and harder punches also have to be taken into consideration.

As soon as the first bell goes, Louis wastes no time in coming forward and letting his hands fly, throwing some beautiful combinations and completely taking Klitschko off guard with his great hand speed.

By the end of the first round Louis has already opened up a nasty cut over Klitschko's left eye. Klitschko is still trying to settle into the fight, but Louis keeps slipping his jabs, getting on the inside and throwing punches in bunches.

By Round Five the difference in skill is really showing. Louis has racked up all the rounds and Klitschko's face is a complete mess with multiple cuts and blood constantly seeping into his eyes. The Ukrainian's lack of inside fighting skill is starting to show, and when up close Louis just has too much firepower.

In between rounds Louis is thinking to himself, Is this guy for real? *He's taken more punishment and been hit with some of the flushest shots he has ever thrown, and yet he's still standing and fighting on, showing no sign of slowing down or quitting.*

The bell goes for Round Six and the Brown Bomber is feeling a little fatigued with the extra effort he's been putting in. Klitschko just keeps coming forward, having now gauged his timing and distance, and is using his jab and right hand to control the range.

When up close Klitschko easily overpowers and outmuscles his smaller foe. Also his leaning on him, holding his head down and general roughhousing is starting to affect Louis.

Towards the end of the round Dr Steelhammer lands a vicious right that dazes Louis, but the bell rings just in time.

Round Seven starts and Klitschko marches forward. His corner have tried their best to stop the bleeding, however the cuts are too deep and too many. It doesn't seem to bother him though; he just comes forward like a Ukrainian Terminator.

Louis is starting to gas and now Klitschko is landing some heavy shots. A big overhand right sends Louis down for the count. He's up at six and covers up for the remainder of the seventh.

Round Eight and again Klitschko is now fully in control of the bout. Louis is struggling with his opponent's power and size. A barrage of hard shots sends Louis down to the canvas again. The Brown Bomber incredibly gets to his feet and bravely continues on.

Into Round Nine and Klitschko is just relentless. A great left hook sends Louis down again. Somehow he battles on, but the ref and corner are all taking a very close look. Towards the end of the round Louis strings together some nice shots and works over Klitschko's face a bit. Blood is now all over Klitschko's shorts and Louis' white gloves have turned a light shade of red.

Round Ten and the commentators are rightly pointing out how Louis is looking very shaky and tired. Right on cue another big right sends Louis down again. He completely forgot to bring back his left after throwing a jab and it's now similar to the Schmeling fight.

Louis is willing to carry on, but the corner waves it off, sparing their fighter. A gruelling fight that was hard to watch at times.

Verdict: TKO win to V. Klitschko in Round Ten.

Co-main Event: Riddick Bowe vs. Sonny Liston

This is the first fight I have had to sleep on before deciding how it will play out. Researching online didn't provide a clear winner, and frankly both are superb heavyweights with some great tools in their arsenal.

Bowe is taller by four inches and heavier by twenty pounds but does give up three inches in reach. Bowe is also the faster fighter and is ahead in terms of heart, stamina and ring IQ.

With a seventy-two percent and seventy-three percent KO ratio respectively, both are formidable punchers. If I had to give the edge in power it would probably go to Liston, but not by a lot. Liston also has the slightly better chin.

Something to note is that even though Liston is fairly short for a heavyweight at six feet one inch, he has a longer reach than anyone else in this book and is freakishly strong. I'm certain Bowe won't be able to outmuscle or push back the Big Bear.

Once things get underway, Liston comes out throwing his stiff ramrod jab and measuring his opponent. Bowe is trying to get up close and land some damaging shots on the inside, but Liston's jab is giving him all sorts of issues.

By the midpoint of the first Bowe is wary of the power his opponent has, not just in his crosses and hooks but also in the stiff jab that keeps throwing Bowe off his rhythm.

The early rounds consist of Liston firing out his piston jab and following it up with some great one-twos. Bowe manages to land some good glancing blows, but nothing too significant. Liston is fighting the perfect fight, taking his time and wearing down his opponent.

By Round Six all the great early work the Big Bear put in is starting to catch up. He's feeling the pace and beginning to slow down, with his punch output also lowering. Bowe notices the deeper breaths his foe is taking and starts to pile on the pressure. When up close he lets his hands go with some great uppercuts and left hooks that rock back Liston's head.

By Round Nine Liston is ahead, six rounds to two, but Bowe doesn't seem to be tiring nearly as fast and is looking to land some real hard shots, swinging almost wildly while looking for the stoppage.

Unawares to Bowe, the Big Bear has gotten his second wind and lands a destructive right that sends Bowe into next week. Bowe is down on the canvas. He staggers to his feet and the ref gives him a close look but allows the fight to continue.

Liston comes in throwing the jab and waiting for the right shot. With thirty seconds to go Bowe is still dazed and Liston lands a violent left hook that knocks Bowe out cold.

Verdict: KO win to Liston in Round Nine.

Main Event: Joe Frazier vs. Mike Tyson

For our main event we have a very personal affair. In 1986 Joe Frazier watched in horror as a ruthless Mike Tyson dispatched of his son Marvis Frazier in just thirty seconds: Tyson's fastest victory of his career.

Frazier is pissed and demands Tyson face him in the ring so he can return the favour. Being an Ali fan, Tyson goads Frazier, saying he will lay the same beating on him.

Once the fight is signed, the animosity between the two is clear. Frazier is coming for Tyson's head and for some reason Ali has joined Tyson's corner as a favour to Cus. Both look to be taking a little too much pleasure in taunting Frazier.

Both fighters are similarly sized. Frazier is an inch taller and has two inches in reach but weighs about ten pounds less. Head-to-head, Tyson clearly hits harder with both hands, is much faster and has the stronger chin, but heart and stamina are firmly in favour of Frazier, who can fight at a blistering pace. Also, Frazier's left hook is probably the best in history and can finish just about anyone.

Smokin' Joe has never wanted to win a fight as badly as he does against Tyson, even more so than against Ali in the Thrilla in Manila. *He's trained extremely diligently and on fight night is in tip-top shape and ready for all-out war.*

Tyson has been fully focused himself and is under no illusion of the task ahead; he's ready and firing on all cylinders.

As the fighters face off the ref is giving his final instructions and Ali is hopping around behind Tyson, shouting at Frazier, calling him a Gorilla and saying anything else that comes into his head.

Cus has to tell him to settle down as he can see the effect it's having on Frazier. To say he's angry is an understatement. He has venom in his eyes and only one thing on his mind: complete annihilation of Tyson.

Everyone has cleared the ring and the bell sounds. Wasting no time, Frazier comes out and goes for broke, completely disregarding all strategy. The first punch is a huge left hook by Frazier that sends Tyson down, – a flash knockdown that Kid Dynamite shakes off and is now pissed himself.

Fighting resumes and Frazier comes gunning in, but Tyson's got his senses and lands a hard jab and follows it up with a nice body shot. They tie up and go into ropes.

Once apart Tyson starts to use his movement and comes in bobbing and weaving, avoiding Frazier's jab and landing a couple of great left hooks then a right uppercut. Frazier feels these and Tyson senses this. Tyson throws a beautiful right to the body and follows it up with a right hook and Frazier is down.

Two knockdowns in the first minute and both fighters are going for broke, fully intending to take the other out.

Frazier gets up and the round continues.

Towards the end of Round One Tyson makes a mental note to avoid Frazier's left hook by either moving to his left or keeping his right hand up and tight to his chin.

In the last thirty seconds of the first both start trading. Frazier is struggling to land his power shots and Iron Mike's firepower is just too much. Frazier eats another uppercut and is forced to take a knee. He gets to his feet and survives the round.

Both fighters are feeling the effects of a frenzied opening and come out for the second raring to go. Tyson's using his superior hand and foot speed to land some excellent combinations that rock Frazier to his boots. Tyson is able to land another hard right which sends Frazier down again for the third time.

Once again, he beats the count and marches forward. Tyson has got his timing down perfectly and with Frazier's come-forward crouching style playing perfectly into his attacks, he's feeling pretty confident. Another left hook sends Smokin' Joe down with ten seconds to go. The bell rings and Frazier stumbles to his corner.

Tyson's corner is telling him not to take his foot off the gas or get complacent, Frazier is an all-time great and always dangerous. "Keep your head about you, use your boxing skills and speed to set up your shots. Don't look for the KO," they urge.

Once Round Three begins Tyson heeds the advice and comes in throwing great jabs, hooks and some brutal uppercuts when up close. Frazier just doesn't have an answer and after suffering another two knockdowns the ref waves the fight off. Frazier is vehemently protesting but Eddie Futch climbs into the ring, consoling his fighter.

Both Tyson and Ali show their respect to their fallen brother and apologise for their behaviour leading up to the fight.

Verdict: TKO win to Tyson in Round Three.

FIGHT CARD FOURTEEN

Jack Dempsey vs. Joe Louis

Sonny Liston vs. Gene Tunney

Riddick Bowe vs. Jack Johnson

Larry Holmes vs. Floyd Patterson

Muhammad Ali vs. Ken Norton

Lennox Lewis vs. Max Schmeling

Vitali Klitschko vs. Jim Jeffries

Wladimir Klitschko vs. Joe Frazier

Co-main Event: Mike Tyson vs. Rocky Marciano

Main Event: George Foreman vs. Evander Holyfield

Jack Dempsey vs. Joe Louis

Kicking off this fight card is a contest that I've surprisingly never considered before, though I'm not sure why as it will be an absolute barn burner with two KO artists who always enter the ring with one goal: to utterly destroy their opponent.

In one corner you have the main man in the division during the roaring twenties against the best fighter in the division during the thirties and forties. Two dominant forces colliding with only one outcome guaranteed: there won't be any need for the judges tonight.

The tale of the tape indicates an evenly balanced pair of boxers. Louis is one inch taller, has three inches in reach and about six pounds in weight; very marginal benefits. In terms of power both hit very hard and could easily knock the other out. Both are fast with their hands, and while Dempsey has the stronger chin; stamina, heart and ring IQ slightly favour Louis.

The build-up to the fight gets a bit spicy with Louis claiming Dempsey has avoided the best Black boxers and is afraid of what he will do to him in the ring. This riles up the Manassa Mauler, who states he is scared of no man and never intentionally avoided anyone; his job is to fight whoever is put in front of him.

A raucous crowd is in the arena tonight, expecting fireworks from the first bell. The crowd is split down the middle with both fighters having large contingencies of fans passionately cheering them on.

Once in the ring neither man takes their eyes off the other. Louis is pacing back and forth while Dempsey stares ahead.

The bell sounds and these two lions are finally unleashed. Dempsey comes charging forward and starts throwing all manner of fast and hard shots, overwhelming Louis and forcing him to tie up.

In between blocking the shots, the odd one slips through and Louis clearly feels the power and ferocity that Dempsey has. Once separated, Louis starts throwing some beautiful combinations and Dempsey is momentarily stunned.

As the round progresses Louis notices Dempsey's lack of technical boxing skills and starts to establish his jab, his fast hands beating Dempsey to the punch.

Round One goes to Louis.

Into the second and again Louis is taking a slightly more measured approach, using his jab to nullify Dempsey's attacks. Dempsey is still having some successes, landing a few hurtful shots, but not enough to truly worry Louis.

The Brown Bomber is already sensing the frustration of his opponent and immediately ups the pace, throwing some blistering three and four-punch combinations that are starting to have an effect.

Round Three and Dempsey is now fully aware of the gap in skills between the two. Under normal circumstances that wouldn't be too much of an issue because Dempsey has two great equalisers – his speed and dynamite in both fists. However, on this night he just happens to be facing a guy who is just as fast and hits just as hard. Dempsey has to get in striking distance to actually land some meaningful punches. The problem he's having is that getting in this position would mean entering Louis' optimal range for his attacks.

During the mid-point of the round Louis has completely taken over and actually knocks Dempsey down with thirty seconds to go. He manages to rise but the next two rounds consist of Louis using his incredible speed, reflexes and power to dismantle Dempsey.

After another knockdown in Round Six the fight is waved off, with Dempsey completely out on his feet.

Verdict: TKO win to Louis in Round Six.

Sonny Liston vs. Gene Tunney

This is an interesting fight. Liston has the clear physical advantage while Tunney has the stylistic edge. Liston struggles a lot with movers and Tunney can box and move for fifteen full rounds. The Fighting Marine also sustained some hard punishment to the body from Dempsey and still continued dancing around the ring, so the question comes down to whether the Big Bear can hurt Tunney enough to finish him off.

The fight will consist of Tunney using his jab, quick feet and lateral movement to stay out of striking distance from Liston. With Liston's long reach and hard jab this won't be an easy task, but Tunney will come into the fight with the perfect game plan, fully prepared for a long tactical fight.

Liston will have successes throughout the twelve rounds and possibly score a knockdown, however Tunney is the favourite and will win most of the rounds to get the decision.

Verdict: Decision win to Tunney.

Riddick Bowe vs. Jack Johnson

Bowe is just too big, hits too hard and his inside fighting is too superior to be troubled by Johnson.

Verdict: TKO win to Bowe in Round Four.

Larry Holmes vs. Floyd Patterson

This will be a very similar fight to the Ali-Patterson matchup. Patterson will show off some great shots via his fast hands and combinations, but Holmes' size, hard jab and skills will prove too much for Patterson down the stretch.

Verdict: TKO win to Holmes in Round Ten.

Muhammad Ali vs. Ken Norton

This is a tricky fight to call. Even though it actually happened three times, the reality is both fighters could win on any given night and Norton always seemed to have Ali's number.

Ali has the official winning record over Norton at two-one, but the last fight was very close and controversial. Many observers argue Norton was robbed and even when I watched the fight, I thought Norton won, but a large part of that was because Ali refused to let his hands go as much as he should have, spending too much time lingering on the ropes and shimmying rather than fighting.

It would be unfair to overrule the result of the winning record and the fights did occur post exile, so Ali had already lost a step and his stamina wasn't quite what it used to be.

An interesting fact is during their fights Norton used to watch Ali's chest rather than his hands or face. By watching his torso he could better anticipate Ali's attacks and counter more effectively.

Verdict: Split decision win to Ali.

Lennox Lewis vs. Max Schmeling

Schmeling, lacking in both the skills and power department, will make this a routine win for Lewis, who is now building towards an epic showdown with Muhammad Ali, the only other fighter to remain undefeated so far.

Verdict: KO win to Lewis in Round Two.

Vitali Klitschko vs. Jim Jeffries

Klitschko is too strong, big and durable for Jeffries to have any success.

Verdict: KO win to V. Klitschko in Round Three.

Wladimir Klitschko vs. Joe Frazier

This is a bad stylistic matchup for Frazier. He is too small and his style will play right into Klitschko's strengths. When up close

Klitschko will just smother Frazier and tie him up, constantly leaning on him and tiring him out.

Most of the fight will consist of Frazier staying out of range on the end of his opponent's stiff hard jab, which will be followed up with debilitating overhand rights.

Verdict: TKO win to W. Klitschko in Round Nine.

Co-main Event: Mike Tyson vs. Rocky Marciano

What a battle this will be. Both come into the fight with the fiercest of reputations as colossal power punchers who never take a backwards step and prefer to finish opponents early and in style.

You have Marciano's formidable chin, two-fisted power, stamina and relentless body attacks going head to head with Tyson's sublime mix of speed and powerful combination punching, as well as his excellent head and foot movement. The come-forward crouching swarmer against Cus' bob and weave style.

Physically both are the same height, while Tyson has three inches in reach and is the heavier fighter in the ring by about twenty pounds.

In terms of power, Marciano has an eighty-eight percent KO ratio, with Tyson coming in at seventy-six percent. All things considered I would say there isn't much between them power-wise. On paper it seems this fight could go either way.

During the press tours both fighters remain respectful and courteous towards each other. This is one of those rare fights that transcends the sport, and casuals take a genuine interest in it, not surprising given the personalities and fan-friendly boxing styles both men possess.

During camp Tyson and Cus watch endless tapes of Marciano and are coming into the fight fully prepared with the perfect game plan: let Marciano walk onto Tyson's punches and take him out early.

Conversely, Marciano has also done his homework and plans to take things cautiously early on and work over Tyson's body, taking him out late in the fight.

Once the bell rings both meet in the centre and Marciano throws a couple of jabs, following it up with a nice right to the body. They both tie up and Tyson is surprised with the strength his foe has, as well as the power in his punches.

Once free Iron Mike comes in bobbing and weaving, letting off a vicious three-punch combination, ending with a cracking left hook to Marciano's chin. The Rock is stunned at the speed and power his opponent has and before he knows it Tyson's flying back in and hitting him with a polarising right uppercut, knocking him down.

Marciano beats the count but Tyson is all over him again, landing another crippling left hook that sends Marciano down again.

The bell sounds and Marciano has got off to a terrible start.

Marciano is slowly recovering but the bell sounds for the second round and, on Cus' urging, Tyson is like a caged animal that's just been unleashed on its prey. He comes forward throwing shots with real spite.

Marciano is just too slow to move out of the way and his chin can't take such huge punches. The Rock goes for broke, throwing a wild left hook which Tyson ducks. When Marciano turns, he doesn't see Tyson's incredible left hook that he's pivoted into.

And *BOOM! Marciano is down and it doesn't look like he's getting up. The count is at six and he's slowly rising, but the ref has seen enough.*

Verdict: TKO win to Tyson in Round Two.

Main Event: George Foreman vs. Evander Holyfield

"Has he just knocked all my teeth out?" Holyfield asked his corner during his fight against George Foreman in 1991. Luckily his teeth were still intact, but Holyfield took some huge power shots in the fight and bravely fought on for twelve hard rounds to claim victory.

For most fights that actually happened I have kept the result the same in this book as it is a little unfair to overturn a win. But on some occasions I have felt compelled to change the result simply because the fight wasn't between both fighters in their primes, for example Louis-Marciano or Ali-Holmes, with both Louis and Ali being well past their best at the time the fights occurred.

Was Foreman past his best when he took on the Real Deal? Absolutely. He was so slow that he made Joe Joyce look as fast as Muhammad Ali.

Now this fight compares Holyfield from 1991 to the Foreman of 1973, a more competitive and even affair.

The strategy employed by Holyfield in this fight will be no different to their actual fight: he will have to keep moving and jabbing, avoiding trouble. The key question is, can it be done against a faster, more efficient and more ruthless Big George Foreman?

The fight starts with Holyfield establishing his jab and staying out of the way of Foreman's hard hooks and huge overhand right. The first couple of rounds go to Holyfield, but Foreman starts cutting the ring off expertly and landing some clubbing blows, dazing his foe.

Once tagged, Holyfield can't help but try and punch his way out of trouble – a bad idea against such a clinical finisher.

In Round Three Holyfield gets tagged and begins trading. Foreman simply waits for the opening and lands a crushing right that sends Holyfield down. Being the warrior that he is, Holyfield rises and beckons his opponent in.

The next two rounds consist of Big George throwing barrages of punches, some of which land but many are blocked. Holyfield's arms and body are now in serious pain, but he puts it to the back of his mind and throws some bombs of his own.

Unfortunately for the Real Deal, his punches just don't have enough pop in them to worry Foreman, who lands a crippling uppercut that buckles Holyfield's knees. Another one-two lands flush and Holyfield is slumped onto the ropes. The corner and ref both simultaneously wave the fight off.

Verdict: TKO win to Foreman in Round Six.

FIGHT CARD FIFTEEN

Joe Frazier vs. Ken Norton

Vitali Klitschko vs. Jack Dempsey

George Foreman vs. Wladimir Klitschko

Max Schmeling vs. Larry Holmes

Evander Holyfield vs. Riddick Bowe

Joe Louis vs. Floyd Patterson

Jim Jeffries vs. Gene Tunney

Rocky Marciano vs. Jack Johnson

Co-main Event: Sonny Liston vs. Mike Tyson

Main Event: Lennox Lewis vs. Muhammad Ali

Joe Frazier vs. Ken Norton

During the golden era of heavyweight boxing in the seventies, Frazier and Norton were two of the biggest names in the division. It is a real shame a fight between the two never happened as it would have been a barn burner with neither man taking a backwards step.

Given that they were stablemates it's understandable why they never fought, however some sparring stories do exist and all point towards Frazier usually coming out on top.

Physically Norton is the bigger man by four inches in height, six-and-a-half inches in reach and a few pounds on Frazier. Both have unreal engines and can fight at pace for the full fifteen rounds. Frazier hits harder (especially with his left hook), and is faster, has a better chin, heart and boxing IQ.

So, once both fighters put their friendship aside and enter combat, how will the fight play out?

Norton comes on strong early doors and establishes his jab, aiming to outmuscle and outwork the smaller fighter. Coming forward with his cross-arm guard he gives Frazier some difficulties and the first two or three rounds comfortably go to Norton.

By Round Four Frazier has settled into the fight and got his timing down while increasing the pressure and punch output, especially to Norton's body. Some vicious hooks from Frazier land flush on Norton and he backs off, looking to tie up.

Late in the round Frazier lands a peach of a left hook that sends his opponent down for the count. However, Norton is one tough SOB and manages to get to his feet, his excellent conditioning coming to his aid as he battles on.

Frazier is like a steam train getting stronger and building momentum with every round. Norton is starting to feel the body shots and is starting to throw less punches, hanging on a bit more in clinches. Frazier is having huge success with constantly slipping under Norton's looping right and following it up with brutal body punches and hooks to the head.

By Round Ten Frazier is in complete control. With his constant pressure and relentless attacks he finally forces Norton's corner to throw in the towel, knowing their fighter has nothing left in the tank.

Verdict: TKO win to Frazier in Round Ten.

Vitali Klitschko vs. Jack Dempsey

A fast and ferocious Dempsey comes out and puts it on Klitschko from the first bell. The first two or three rounds go to Dempsey, however he doesn't really hurt his taller foe, only succeeding in annoying him.

Once Klitschko starts controlling the ring and landing some bombs of his own, the massive size difference comes into effect. Every time they tie up, Klitschko's huge bulk drains the Manassa Mauler of his strength.

With the Ukrainian's iron chin he rides out any early rough patches and by the mid-point of the fight he finally puts Dempsey down and out for the count.

Verdict: KO win to V. Klitschko in Round Six.

George Foreman vs. Wladimir Klitschko

Klitschko comes into this fight knowing the only strategy is to use his jab, movement and grabbing to completely frustrate Big George. In the early rounds Klitschko has some good success in controlling the pace and not getting hit flush, however Foreman eventually breaks through. Once he lands a huge right, Dr Steelhammer isn't able to recover.

Verdict: TKO win to Foreman in Round Five.

Max Schmeling vs. Larry Holmes

Schmeling brings nothing to the table that will worry Holmes, with his superior skills, size and movement this will be a relatively easy night's work for the Easton Assassin.

Verdict: Decision win to Holmes.

Evander Holyfield vs. Riddick Bowe

We don't need to hypothesise how this would have gone; these two amazing warriors gave us perhaps the greatest trilogy of fights in boxing. Bowe came out on top two-one and since both were in their primes, the result stands.

Verdict: Decision win to Bowe.

Joe Louis vs. Floyd Patterson

Patterson is not good enough to avoid Louis' combinations and he definitely doesn't have the chin to withstand the punishment the Brown Bomber will dish out.

Verdict: KO win to Louis in Round Two.

Jim Jeffries vs. Gene Tunney

Tunney is too skilled, too slick and too fast to lose a round to the slow Jeffries.

Verdict: Decision win to Tunney.

Rocky Marciano vs. Jack Johnson

Johnson will use his defensive prowess to keep Marciano at bay, however his low punch output and lack of power will let him down. Marciano will just walk straight through whatever Johnson tries and work over his body, mixing in some powerful shots upstairs.

Verdict: TKO win to Marciano in Round Six.

Co-main Event: Sonny Liston vs. Mike Tyson

Just imagine you're in the school playground and the two toughest, meanest bullies who normally are cordial to each other finally snap, and it's about to kick off. Kids from across the playground come streaming in and, in unison, start chanting "FIGHT! FIGHT! FIGHT!"

Now consider that rather than a playground, you have the squared circle and in each corner, you have two of the most feared and intimidating bullies in boxing history.

In the red corner there's Sonny Liston, with his stint in prison and connections to the criminal underworld, staring a hole through Mike Tyson, who was born and raised on the unforgiving streets of Brooklyn, New York, spent time in youth correctional facilities and had three years behind bars. Neither man fears the other and neither can wait for the bell to ring.

Both fighters are physical specimens. Liston is taller by three inches, both weigh around the same and Liston also has a huge thirteen-inch reach advantage – the biggest gap of any two fighters in this book. However, Tyson won't be too fussed about the size difference; he is used to being the shorter man and his peek-a-boo style actually plays into his short, powerful arms.

In terms of power, I would say it's even. Tyson is much faster and more explosive, whereas Liston is the stronger of the two and more controlled in his methodical approach. Liston has the stronger chin, more heart and better stamina, with their ring IQ being about even.

The bell rings and everyone watching takes in a deep, collective breath, waiting for the fireworks. Tyson comes storming out with only one goal in mind: to take Liston's head off. He bobs and weaves his way in, letting off some ferocious body shots and hooks to the Big Bear's head.

Liston grabs hold of Tyson and both stagger into the ropes. Liston is impressed with the speed and power of his foe, but has no problems moving him around and controlling the clinch.

Tyson gets his left free and BOOM! A huge hook sends Liston reeling into the corner. Another overhand right blasts him flush on the chin and Liston is down and hurt. As the ref counts, Liston rises to his feet and shakes off the cobwebs. Liston is now fully alert to the danger of one misstep.

The round ends just in time, and both make their way to their respective corners. Tyson is feeling good, but Liston is enraged, refusing any water or to listen to any advice from his corner. He's steaming and ready to bring the fight.

Round Two starts, and Liston settles his feet and starts firing off his ramrod jab. Each time he lets it go it hits the target and resets Tyson's rhythm. Liston mixes in some rights and left hooks and is working his way back into the fight.

Tyson is still bobbing his way in and landing some nice glancing blows, but nothing too telling. Liston covers up each time Tyson gets up close.

Round Three and Liston comes out again behind his jab, throwing some hard rights that connect. Tyson ducks under a jab and comes up on the inside with a decapitating uppercut that rocks Liston to the core, breaking his nose in the process. With blood pouring out his nose, breathing is proving to be difficult.

In between rounds Liston asks his corner how his nose looks and his trainer Willie Reddish replies that it is an improvement. This is all Liston needs to hear to spur him on. He comes out and keeps the left jab firmly in Tyson's face. Each time Tyson tries to slip it, Liston throws a right and ties things up.

The long reach of the Big Bear is proving to be difficult to outmanoeuvre and the constant hard shots Tyson is eating are starting to take a toll.

In Round Five Tyson is starting to feel frustrated while Liston just seems to get stronger. Tyson has used up a lot of energy working his way into position to throw his deadly shots, and while coming in has had to absorb quite a bit of punishment.

Towards the end of the round Liston pushes Tyson off him and lands a stunning right that knocks Kid Dynamite down. He manages to get back up and see out the round.

The next two rounds take a similar pattern, with Liston taking his time, relying on his jab, strength and fundamentals to control the pace. Tyson is starting to get a little desperate and starts throwing some wild shots, but none land.

Round Eight and Tyson has drastically slowed down. His punches lack the snap of earlier in the fight and with a swollen left eye he's looking pretty dejected. Liston steps up the pressure, sensing the end is near, and lands with a barrage of unanswered blows that force the ref to jump in and end proceedings.

Verdict: TKO win to Liston in Round Eight.

Main Event: Lennox Lewis vs. Muhammad Ali

This is the fight we've all been waiting for; the only remaining undefeated fighters in the book going head-to-head, both coming into the fight with a perfect fourteen-zero record. Whoever comes out on top could very well go on to finish the winner of this fantasy league.

Two of the most perfect heavyweight fighters to ever exist, Lewis defeated every man he stepped into the ring with, and Ali was the first ever three-time heavyweight champion and clearly the best fighter of the golden age during the seventies.

Head-to-head Lewis is the taller fighter by two inches, has a six-inch reach advantage and about thirty-five pounds on Ali. Lewis also hits harder, with a seventy-two percent KO ratio against Ali's sixty percent.

The Lion is also the more technical fighter with great boxing skills, however Ali's flaws are intentional; he purposely leaves his hands low and pulls back from punches to be in a better position to counter, and with his lightning-fast reflexes this isn't too much of an issue.

Ali is much faster with hand speed, the likes of which Lewis has never experienced. He is also faster on his feet, easily coming in and out of range. Ali also has the better chin and stamina.

They are about even in heart, with perhaps the slight edge going to the American. In terms of ring IQ they are two of the smartest fighters ever to step in the ring. Lewis has a grandmaster of chess-like approach, with Ali being able to adapt to all manner of situations and come up with winning strategies mid-fight.

This battle is difficult to pick a clear winner for. If they fought ten times it could very well end in five wins each.

The only venue with the prestige and history that could host such a spectacular contest is Madison Square Garden, which sells out in record time. All manner of celebrities are attending to witness history in the making in a true showcase of the immortals.

Neither camp is difficult during the negotiations and the fight is agreed and signed without too much fuss. With the ink barely dry Ali starts his mind games, taunting Lewis and trying to get under his skin. Both fighters are fully aware of the other's strengths and are under no illusion as to the task at hand.

During the press conference to announce the date Ali constantly taunts his opponent, making bold and almost lubricious claims of an early KO. He even recites one of his famous poems:

Sorry fans but I have to tell ya

Lennox Lewis is a phoney

He's thirty-six, unmarried and pretty lonely

I have a prediction of his fate

He will fall in Round Eight.

As soon as he finishes there is uproar from Lewis' trainers, handlers and all manner of hangers-on, who start some pushing and shoving. Lewis himself isn't too happy with the implications and threatens to fight Ali there and then.

Luckily security breaks things up and with the public's interest heightened further (if that was even possible) we have a super main event and the biggest fight in the book about to get underway.

With a full twelve-week camp ahead of them, everyone settles in for perhaps the most important three months of their lives.

Holed up in Deer Lake, Ali and his trainer Angelo Dundee are fully-focused and training harder than ever, constantly reviewing Lewis' fight tapes and discussing all manner of possibilities within the fight.

Lewis is also diligently training at the famous Kronk Gym with Emmanuel Steward again analysing tape after tape of Ali's fights.

Both camps feel confident with their strategies and believe they have found the key weaknesses in the other's armour. This can also be seen as a battle of two of the greatest trainers, with Dundee squaring off against Steward.

During the weigh-in Ali is at his bombastic best, shouting all manner of obscenities towards his foe. But under Steward's instructions, Lewis doesn't even acknowledge Ali's words. A zen-like Lewis is fully focused and in the zone, avoiding falling into the trap of letting Ali get into his head. If anything, Ali is a bit perturbed himself at the lack of reaction but is full of confidence going in and ready for war.

The odds are dead even with the bookies and pundits unable to pick a favourite. A true fifty/fifty fight if there ever was one.

With the fans seated, Michael Buffer gets things underway:

"Introducing to you first from London, England weighing 249 pounds and a record of forty-one wins, two defeats and one draw … the Lion, Lennox Lewis! And his opponent from Kentucky, USA weighing 214 pounds and with a record of fifty-six wins, five defeats and no draws, the Greatest, Muhammad Ali!"

Applause and cheering for both fighters echoes throughout the arena. A large contingency of UK fans made the trip over the Atlantic to support their fellow countryman and are at their rambunctious best.

The bell sounds and we are off. Both fighters come out tentatively and begin the early process of sizing each other up. Ali fires off some lightning-quick jabs and combinations, then dances out of position before Lewis can really land anything.

Lewis settles in and begins launching his piston jab each time Ali gets within range, leveraging his longer reach to control the distance. A glancing right lands for Lewis as the best punch of the round.

Round Two and Lewis comes out throwing a few more punches. Both fighters have loosened up and are letting their hands go while still remaining cautious. Every time they tie up Lewis is using his bulk to weigh down his foe, pushing Ali's head down and employing some roughhouse tactics. The ref has to warn Lewis to clean things up before he is forced to take a point.

Another pretty uneventful round that goes to the Lion.

Round Three and Ali is having problems with getting close enough to actually land, with Lewis covering up well or just smothering Ali's work. A few hard punches land for Lewis and he takes another round.

The game plan is working perfectly for the Englishman, though towards the end of the round Ali picks up a few tells on when to anticipate the jab or right and has made a mental note.

Round Four and a split second before Lewis is about to throw his jab, BOOM! A huge right from Ali stuns Lewis and is followed by a beautiful three-punch combination that sends Lewis reeling. He has no idea what has hit him.

As he is trying to regain his senses, Ali moves in and lands a rapid left jab, then a right and a left hook and another right, all within four seconds. Lewis careens into the blue corner, looking befuddled.

As Ali comes marching in, Lewis grabs hold and both wrestle for ten seconds before the ref steps in.

Lewis is covering up tight and aiming to get to the end of the round while his foe is looking for openings and throwing all manner of punches. Even the glancing shots are starting to sting.

The round ends and Lewis is shaken up. Emanuel Steward pleads with Lewis to take a round or two off to regain his footing in the fight, otherwise he will be blown away, reasoning that there is no point trading with someone so much faster than you if your legs aren't steady.

Lewis wisely follows said advice and Ali easily wins the next two rounds from sheer activity, but can't seem to land any telling blows, with Lewis firmly on the defensive. After six rounds the fight is dead even.

During the break before Round Seven Lewis has fully recovered and is ready. Steward simply tells him it's time to bring out the secret weapon. Through their analysis of Ali's fights it was plainly obvious that he has a clear weakness: a tendency to be hit with the left. So, for months in camp the Lion and his trainer diligently practiced and honed the perfect antidote to Ali's immense strengths: a devastating left hook. The initial plan was to bring it out earlier in the fight, but with Lewis' tumultuous last three rounds Emmanuel felt it best to wait.

The bell sounds for Round Seven and Lewis comes out with extra vigour. He waits for Ali to dance into range and BOOM! He lands a brutal left hook out of nowhere. His opponent was not expecting this and is staggering. Another left hook misses and they both tie up.

Ali whispers in Lewis' ear, "Is that all you got, sucka?" and when they break another hard left lands for Lewis. Ali is backed into the ropes.

Lewis doesn't go in for the kill, preferring to control the rest of the round and not take too many risks.

Rounds Eight and Nine are in Lewis' favour with Ali slowing and having big problems with the jab and now a left hook that makes his head spin whenever it lands. Lewis' power is really showing and whenever he goes on the attack Ali has to move out of position.

Lewis is impressed with the punishment his opponent is taking, convinced any other man would have long tasted the canvas.

Round Ten and we are into the championship rounds. Ali comes out dancing and throwing some beautiful combinations. He circles to his left to avoid the hook while also throwing more punches. Knowing he's behind on the cards he lets his hands go and outlands Lewis three-one.

Round Eleven and Ali comes out throwing some great combos. Lewis lands some hard jabs and towards the middle of the round lands a huge left hook that slows Ali down for about a minute. By the last thirty seconds Ali's head has cleared he lets some great shots rip.

A difficult round to score with both fighters having good successes.

Round Twelve and the crowd is on their feet cheering on both warriors and encouraging them to give it their all for the final round. Ali comes out dancing, landing a great jab, right uppercut, left hook then an overhand right that gets the crowd oohing.

Both fighters are trying to finish strong and impress the judges, with Ali's adjustments and fast hands allowing him to win most exchanges. Lewis does land some good shots of his own, but the round goes to Ali, who fought like his life depended on it.

The bell rings and the fighters embrace. The crowd is ecstatic at having witnessed a brilliant boxing match between two of the greatest heavyweight fighters to have lived.

The judges are taking extra long to give their verdict and with the crowd now hushed the decision reads...

Verdict: Split Decision win to Lewis.

Summary: Fight Cards Eleven to Fifteen

O ur last stop before the final four fight cards is complete. The biggest talking point is obviously the epic encounter between Lennox Lewis and Muhammad Ali, the only two undefeated fighters left, and with Lewis coming out the victor he has positioned himself perfectly to win the league.

However looking at both fighters' upcoming schedules, Lewis winning isn't a foregone conclusion as he is yet to fight George Foreman, Larry Holmes, Mike Tyson or Wladimir Klitschko – all tough fights with four boxers currently in the top ten.

Ali, on the other hand, has a relatively easier schedule with George Foreman, Jim Jeffries, Joe Louis and Max Schmelling. The only tough fight will be against Louis, with Ali having already beaten Foreman. So anything can happen.

The top five has remained unchanged from the end of Fight Card Ten and if boxers from sixth to tenth place don't start recording some wins, we could very well be looking at the top five boxers.

In other changes, Vitali Klitschko has jumped from twelfth to sixth. With a great run of wins and with both brothers on thirty points we could be setting up a mouth-watering showdown between siblings.

Some of the best fights from these last five cards were:

- Joe Louis vs. Lennox Lewis
- Sonny Liston vs. Mike Tyson
- Lennox Lewis vs. Muhammad Ali
- Sonny Liston vs. Riddick Bowe

Current League Standings After Fifteen Fight Cards

		Wins	Losses	Draws	Points
1	Lennox Lewis	17			45
2	Muhammad Ali	16	1		42
3	George Foreman	13	2		39
4	Mike Tyson	12	3		36
5	Sonny Liston	10	5		30
6	Vitali Klitschko	10	5		30
7	Wladimir Klitschko	10	5		30
8	Joe Louis	9	6		27
9	Larry Holmes	9	6		27
10	Evander Holyfield	8	7		24
11	Joe Frazier	8	7		24
12	Riddick Bowe	8	7		24
13	Gene Tunney	5	10		15
14	Rocky Marciano	5	10		15
15	Jack Dempsey	4	11		12
16	Ken Norton	4	11		12
17	Max Schmeling	2	13		6

18	Floyd Patterson	1	14		3
19	Jack Johnson	1	14		3
20	Jim Jeffries	1	14		3

Let's bring on the next four cards and crown the undisputed best heavyweight in history.

FIGHT CARD SIXTEEN

Evander Holyfield vs. Mike Tyson

Jack Johnson vs. Sonny Liston

Floyd Patterson vs. Gene Tunney

Ken Norton vs. Riddick Bowe

Joe Frazier vs. Larry Holmes

Max Schmeling vs. Vitali Klitschko

Rocky Marciano vs. Wladimir Klitschko

Jim Jeffries vs. Jack Dempsey

Co-main Event: Lennox Lewis vs. George Foreman

Main Event: Joe Louis vs. Muhammad Ali

Evander Holyfield vs. Mike Tyson

Even though this fight has happened twice, with Holyfield winning both contests, Tyson was clearly not at his best, with the stint in prison having affected his skills. After his incarceration Tyson did put together four wins, but all opponents were hand-picked to make Tyson look as good as possible. Looking back, you can clearly see the decline, so it would be unfair to use the results from their two fights.

It is a shame the fight didn't happen in 1991 as planned, but to be honest even then Tyson wasn't the same fighter and most likely would have lost. Too much partying and neglecting training was starting to have a clear effect on his boxing, and coming up against a young, hungry and focused Real Deal would have been bad news for Tyson.

So here we have Tyson from 1987 against Holyfield from 1992, a perfectly balanced fight between two gladiators at the peak of their powers.

Physically, Holyfield is the bigger man with four inches in height and six inches in reach over Tyson. In terms of weight both are even at a trim and ready 218 pounds.

Holyfield has the heart, stamina and ring IQ while Iron Mike clearly hits harder and is faster. Both are about equal when it comes to chin.

Once the bell goes Tyson comes out faster, throwing all manner of punches and looking to take out his adversary early. Holyfield is fully prepared for the onslaught and rides out a couple of rough rounds, taking some punishment.

Once into the third Holyfield starts putting his shots together and with his subtle but effective use of his head, he starts bullying Tyson. The Real Deal has a tendency to trade a little too often and gets caught with some big shots from Tyson, but his tough chin and unreal heart carries him through any rough patches.

By the mid rounds Holyfield has fully taken over the fight with an out-of-sorts Tyson getting more desperate by the minute. Holyfield keeps the jab in his foe's face and at least once per round he manoeuvres his head into position to butt Tyson and frustrate him further.

By Round Ten Tyson is cut over both eyes, ruled as a result of accidental clashes of the head – something hotly contested by Tyson's corner. Holyfield comes out piling on the pressure and by the end of the round senses the end is near.

In Round Eleven Tyson goes for broke, swinging wildly, however Holyfield is ready and as soon as he spots an opening throws a barrage of his own hard punches that knocks Tyson down. He struggles to his feet, but another assault and the ref waves it off.

Some fighters just have another's number and sadly Holyfield is Tyson's bogeyman.

Verdict: TKO win to Holyfield in Round Eleven.

Jack Johnson vs. Sonny Liston

Johnson has the defensive skills to keep Liston away for a couple of rounds, but eventually the Big Bear will find a way through. When he lands clean it will be lights out for Johnson.

Verdict: KO win to Liston in Round Three.

Floyd Patterson vs. Gene Tunney

A tricky fight to pick a winner for, as both boxers have great strengths and with no clear size advantage this will be an exciting and fast-paced clash.

Patterson brings tremendous hand speed and a difficult bob and weave style. Tunney is a great boxing technician with excellent footwork and defensive skills.

Tunney does hit pretty hard, but most of his knockouts are guys smaller than him. Will he be able to hurt and finish the faster fighter? Most likely no, so we will have a twelve-round battle with some sublime boxing on display and both fighters showing great heart to continue fighting on.

Once Tunney figures out Patterson's style and makes some adjustments I can see him winning more exchanges and controlling the fight, especially since Patterson likes to linger in position between attacks; the Fighting Marine will definitely take advantage of this.

Verdict: Decision win to Tunney.

Ken Norton vs. Riddick Bowe

Norton's cross-arm defence will play into Bowe's inside game, and with the big size difference and Bowe's powerful uppercuts, Norton's chin just won't hold up.

Verdict: TKO win to Bowe in Round Four.

Joe Frazier vs. Larry Holmes

This is a main event fight in its own right and it is a shame the fight never happened during the seventies.

Stylistically you have Joe Frazier, the come-forward brawler with relentless body punching, unlimited stamina and a show-stopping left hook, going up against the silky-smooth boxing skills of Larry Holmes with his superb left jab, excellent fundamentals, fast hands and feet. A true clash of styles where both fighters will have their moments.

Holmes has just seen what Frazier did to Ali in the Fight of the Century *and is seeking revenge for his idol and sparring partner. Holmes demands Frazier meet him face to face in the middle of the ring to pay penance for the sin of beating Ali. Frazier is more than happy to oblige and the fight is set.*

A lot can actually be gained from studying the *Fight of the Century*. Ali, who was faster than Holmes, wasn't able to keep Frazier off him and absorbed untold punishment to the body. Holmes was slower than Ali, didn't have the same endurance or reflexes and was not known to be a power puncher. His KO ratio was fifty-nine percent; pretty much the same as Ali's at sixty percent.

So, the question is, can the Easton Assassin keep Frazier off him long enough to land his own crisp shots? All things considered, most likely no.

Holmes gets off to an early start, winning the first four rounds against his opponent's traditional slow start, however once Frazier settles into the fight he constantly applies the pressure with hard, powerful shots to the body and a swift left hook to Holmes' chin.

Each time the hook connects, Holmes feels it and has to hold on. After twelve tough, hard-fought rounds Frazier comes out ahead, eight rounds to four.

Verdict: Decision win to Frazier.

Max Schmeling vs. Vitali Klitschko

Klitschko will control the centre of the ring and once Schmeling gives his much bigger foe an opening Dr Ironfist will blast Schmeling into next week.

Verdict: KO win to V. Klitschko in Round Three.

Rocky Marciano vs. Wladimir Klitschko

Marciano definitely has the style and power to cause Klitschko issues, but the massive size and skill difference is glaring. Klitschko will be literally towering over the Rock with eight inches in height, fifty pounds in weight and fourteen inches in reach. A very physically unbalanced fight.

Dr Steelhammer will take his time and use his superior boxing skills to time Marciano. Once he starts landing with his sledgehammer right the fight can only go one way from there.

Verdict: TKO win to W. Klitschko in Round Six.

Jim Jeffries vs. Jack Dempsey

Jeffries is just a little too slow and crude to avoid Dempsey's ferocious attacks. Once Dempsey has Jeffries going he won't let up until his foe is down and out.

Verdict: KO win to Dempsey in Round Three.

Co-main Event: Lennox Lewis vs. George Foreman

Here we have the master tactician Lennox Lewis colliding head-on with a brutal *throw bombs first and ask questions later* George Foreman. Two big, strong hard-hitting heavies in their primes going head-to-head.

Can Foreman land clean on Lewis? Will Lewis simply out jab and out box Big George? If Foreman lands, can Lewis' chin hold up?

A fascinating match-up.

When Foreman made his great comeback in the nineties, he specifically avoided a tussle with both Lewis and Bowe, and for obvious reasons. Both fighters hit hard and were in their primes; not a good idea to go up against them at over forty and being much slower. However, a prime Foreman from 1973 will have no issue with stepping into the ring with the Lion and will look to tame him.

Physically both are specimens, with Foreman standing at six feet three-and-a-half inches and Lewis being slightly taller at six feet five inches. Lewis also has the longer reach by five inches and weighs about twenty-five pounds more on the night. A potentially big advantage.

Both fighters are superior power punchers and pack some serious dynamite. Foreman hits the harder of the two and is the better finisher. Chin is also in the American's favour, but heart, stamina and ring IQ all heavily sway towards Lewis.

Going into the fight, both fighters will have a distinct strategy. Foreman will look to hurt Lewis early and, in an ideal world, end the fight within five or six rounds.

Lewis will look to stay behind his jab and use his boxing skills to take the fight into the latter rounds, either securing a comfortable points win or stop a tired Big George. Lewis will have to box the perfect fight and not place one foot wrong, otherwise it could be lights out as he enters a Category Five hurricane.

Once the bell rings both fighters come out and touch gloves as a sign of respect. Then we are off.

A stiff jab from Lewis lands, followed by a hard right. Lewis is fully aware of the danger his opponent brings and is boxing very carefully. When up close Lewis ties Foreman up and tries to rough him up, however Foreman is the stronger of the two and easily holds his own when.

A few glancing blows land for the Lion with a couple of hard shots from Foreman to the body that find their target. Nothing too spectacular but the round goes to Lewis.

Round Two and again Lewis calmly approaches things and stays behind the jab, throwing some nice uppercuts when on the inside. Foreman absorbs them but notes he can't take too many of these punches, otherwise he could be the one getting knocked out. A grim thought that ignites a fire within him. The round goes to Lewis.

The bell sounds for the third and this time Foreman has a slight spring in his step. He's biting on his gum shield extra hard and going hell for leather. He masterfully cuts off the ring and, with Lewis in position, fires a deadly left hook/jab while walking forward. Lewis is caught completely off guard and before he can react a pulverising overhand right from Foreman sends Lewis crashing to the canvas.

Using the ropes to rise, the Englishman beats the count and Foreman comes powering in, throwing a barrage of shots. Lewis holds on, trying to see out the round.

However, there is too much time left and Foreman is in the zone. Another right to the temple sends Lewis down and he's struggling, a dazed look in his eyes. He again manages to get to his feet and the bell sounds.

The commentators suggest that if Lewis doesn't recover fast, this could be the last round.

Round Four and an eager Foreman carelessly swings away, but Lewis lands a superb right bang on the chin and Foreman is seeing stars. Another left hook from Lewis and Foreman is now tasting the canvas. What a turnaround!

The crowd is going wild and the ref is at six but Foreman isn't done yet. He makes the count and nods to Lewis. Lewis has found his legs and is ready for war. Knowing he can't withstand too many Foreman bombs, he comes in looking to take out his foe. This has become a wild brawl with both putting everything into their punches, looking for one big blow to end things.

With thirty seconds to go Lewis lands a decapitating right uppercut that sends Foreman flying into the corner. Lewis charges in but walks right into a left hook and he's now staggering. It's like watching two drunks throwing dukes outside a bar. The crowd is enthralled at such a fast-paced, exciting fight. Both fighters bravely stay on their feet and manage to hear the bell.

In between rounds Lewis' corner plead that he revert back to the original game plan: fight from behind the jab and stop entering exchanges unnecessarily. Lewis comes out, trying to establish his jab, but Foreman is just too strong and breaks through, landing a clubbing right that Lewis is forced to hold on from.

Once separated, Big George connects with another left hook and this time it's one too many. Lewis is hanging on but with two minutes still to go Foreman piles on the pressure and manages to land a thudding left that sends the Lion down again.

As he's battling to his feet the ref has finally seen enough and waves off the fight. An absolute barn burner with both fighters giving as good as they got.

Verdict: TKO win to Foreman in Round Five.

Main Event: Joe Louis vs. Muhammad Ali

If you asked any boxing historian or aficionado who they consider to be the best heavyweight of all time, the two most common names mentioned would be Joe Louis and Muhammad Ali. If there was a Mount Rushmore of heavyweight greats, Louis and Ali would be the first two picks without question.

Both bring the highest level of achievements ever seen in the division. With Louis having enjoyed a twelve-year reign as champ with a record-setting twenty-five title defences, he was head and shoulders above his contemporaries. Ali, on the other hand, was the first ever three-time world heavyweight champion, three-time lineal world heavyweight champion, Olympic gold medallist and the best fighter of his respective era, which was dubbed the "golden years" for the division. Visiting either fighter's trophy room would require sunglasses.

Surprisingly there are quite a few career parallels between these two greats. During their best years Louis and Ali defeated the best competition available and avenged all losses.

Each fighter was enlisted to serve in the military. Louis acquiesced and the infamous "bum of the month" was coined for all the sub-par fighters he crushed while entertaining the troops. Ali decided to refuse participation and was stripped of his title, licence and lost three years of his career.

Towards the end of their careers both suffered a couple of defeats they were unable to avenge and both Louis and Ali were able to pass the torch to the next generation's dominant fighter in Marciano and Holmes, respectively.

Looking at the tale of the tape Ali is an inch taller and has two inches in reach but, more importantly, has twenty pounds in weight over his opponent.

In terms of power, Louis is the much harder hitter with dynamite in both fists. He also has fast hands and excellent combination punching.

Ali definitely has much faster feet. For hand speed I would also give the edge to Ali, but it is close. Chin and ring IQ are also in

Ali's favour, with stamina and heart pretty much equal between the two.

The fight will come down to Ali's speed and movement versus Louis' powerful combination punching and finishing ability.

The fight brings huge international attention with politicians, celebrities and the like all clamouring for a ticket to what some are describing as the most monumental boxing fight in the history of the sport.

There has never been a contest among two fighters who dominated their divisions for such long periods. Louis was the man in the thirties and forties and he is colliding with the best fighter of the sixties and seventies. A true generational battle that transcends the sport and will easily be the most watched sporting event in history.

Pundits are analysing this fight meticulously and sixty percent are leaning towards an Ali win, but no one is picking with confidence and the bookies are taking a record number of bets.

The showdown is booked for the MGM Grand in Las Vegas, with fans flocking from around the world to witness history in the making.

With the fans seated, the National Anthem finishes and the MC begins: "Ladies and Gentlemen, introducing first from Louisville, Kentucky, USA, weighing 214 pounds: the Greatest, Muhammad Ali!"

The crowd erupts as he makes his way to the ring, security pushing back rabid fans just trying to touch him. Ali has his fight face on. There is no acknowledgement of the crowd and no smiles, just pure focus on the task at hand. He enters and lifts a customary hand in the air to gesture to the crowd. They eat it up, cheering, whooping and going wild for their favourite.

The MC continues: "Now from Chambers County, Alabama, USA, weighing 194 pounds: the Brown Bomber, Joe Louis!"

On cue the crowd cheer and holler for Louis as he methodically makes his way to the ring. The commentators compare the look on his face to the same one he had during the rematch against Max Schmeling: complete and utter focus; an almost tunnel vision on the task at hand.

Once instructions are complete, both fighters walk to their corners, take off their robes and the bell rings.

Commentator Jim Lampley observes that he has never seen a crowd at fever pitch before a punch has even been thrown. Fans for both fighters are chanting in unison, "Louis! Ali! Louis! Ali!" Trumpets are blowing in a wild and frenzied atmosphere.

The first round begins with both fighters coming out cautiously and pawing their jabs while finding their range. Neither commits too much and are clearly wary of the man in front of them.

Ali starts dancing and circling Louis, throwing his fast jab and following it up with some quickfire shots, then evading the response.

Louis is impressed with the hand and foot speed his foe possesses and is struggling to get a read on things. It doesn't help that each time he gets close enough to throw his own bombs, Ali effortlessly glides out of position. Louis has already noticed the so-called errors in Ali's style – leaving his hands low and pulling back from punches – but every time he tries to capitalise, he misses and is met with an onslaught of stinging shots, most of which he can't see.

Thankfully they don't hurt too much, but it's already starting to annoy him.

The first round is clearly Ali's. Louis' corner plead with him to rely on his jab and not to chase him, but to let Ali approach him.

While Louis is trying to get a rhythm going, the Greatest is simply sticking to his own game plan: no trading shots, stick and move. Ali's foot speed is really showing, with the Brown Bomber just not able to get close enough.

Rounds Two to Five are all Ali's, who easily dominates proceedings with his beautiful combinations and movement. During a clinch Ali winds up his opponent, saying, "I thought you would be better. You hit like a girl."

Round Six and Ali is starting to take his foot off the gas, not dancing around as much and lingering in dangerous positions a bit too long. Louis is more than happy to take advantage and starts throwing some blistering combinations. A hard left hook rocks Ali's head back and forces him to tie up. Louis is starting to cut the ring off more effectively and senses his chance to get back into the fight.

Rounds Seven to Nine go to Louis, who seems to be getting stronger. He ploughs forward and manoeuvres Ali into the corner, then throws some vicious punches. A left jab, right cross and a left hook all land clean, forcing Ali to hold. Still, he shakes his head and signals to the crowd that that was nothing.

Towards the end of Round Nine, with Ali against the ropes, a crunching left hook from Louis lands on the button and Ali falls back into the ropes and is down. With the ref at five he manages to get to his feet and has a defiant, if not wary, look on his face.

Louis comes in and lands a couple of hard shots, but Ali is too smart. He holds effectively and smothers Louis' work to see out the round.

With the knockdown the fight has tipped in Louis' favour and with three rounds to go it's anyone's fight. Ali's corner is screaming at him to wake up and go back to the game plan or else he'll lose the biggest fight of his career.

Ali shakes his head, rises and beckons Louis in while grandstanding to the crowd. As requested, Louis comes out looking to end things, but Ali has recovered and is in no mood to mess around. He's back on his feet, dancing and firing his jab while following it up with some nice combinations that come in like a whip.

Louis is tiring and with his leaky defence is eating way too many shots. An overhand right from Ali stuns Louis, but he manages to stay on his feet.

Into Round Eleven and Ali is getting stronger. The commentators can't believe where he's found the energy, still throwing punches with the same frequency he did in the opening round. Again, Louis is just too slow footed to land anything significant and Ali just peppers him for the duration of the round.

The final round and both fighters are feeling the effects of a tough, hard-fought fight, but being the absolute warriors they are, the thought of losing or retreating never crosses either's mind. Instead, both come out looking to finish the fight in style.

Louis is throwing everything at Ali. His punches still pack a whole lot of venom and when he manages to land some nice one-two shots, Ali covers up, knowing another knockdown could swing the fight.

Once Louis finishes his combination Ali throws his own, landing three out of four punches. With the crowd reacting to every punch that lands, the atmosphere is electric.

Both fighters land meaningful shots and the round could go either way. The bell sounds and both embrace, informing the other they are the best fighter they've ever faced.

Verdict: Split Decision win to Ali.

FIGHT CARD SEVENTEEN

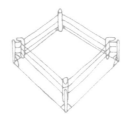

Riddick Bowe vs. Joe Louis

Sonny Liston vs. Floyd Patterson

Jack Johnson vs. Ken Norton

Gene Tunney vs. Joe Frazier

Larry Holmes vs. Rocky Marciano

Muhammad Ali vs. Jim Jeffries

Wladimir Klitschko vs. Evander Holyfield

Jack Dempsey vs. Max Schmeling

Co-main Event: Vitali Klitschko vs. George Foreman

Main Event: Mike Tyson vs. Lennox Lewis

Riddick Bowe vs. Joe Louis

The opening bout to Fight Card Seventeen is a blockbuster. You have the Brown Bomber going toe to toe with his fellow countryman, Big Daddy Riddick Bowe. Both fighters are evenly matched and bring some real strengths and firepower to the contest. Such a closely contested fight will come down to fine margins, and one mistake could end proceedings.

Physically Bowe is the bigger man by three inches in height, forty pounds in weight and five inches in reach. Bowe has a sturdier chin and slightly higher ring IQ and inside fighting ability, too. On balance Louis hits the harder of the two and throws the faster, deadlier combinations. He also has faster hands, more heart and better stamina.

The power on display will be unreal and such a fight is unlikely to see the final bell.

Once the fight begins Louis comes out throwing some beautiful combinations and tearing into Bowe's chin. Bowe is taken aback by his opponent's hand speed and the sting his punches are leaving. He's forced to cover up and hold for the first round.

Louis comes out for the second and lets his punches rip. Knowing his opponent's defensive weak points, he's finding the target too often. Bowe is taking some painful shots and can't seem to find an answer.

In between rounds Bowe's corner plead with him to wake up and take the fight to his foe. They encourage him to get up close, throw his punches on the inside and use his size when in a clinch.

On cue he comes out and heeds the advice, taking the fight up close and landing some nice uppercuts on the inside, then tying Louis up. Each time they clinch Bowe leans and holds a bit more than he usually does, which starts to enrage the Brown Bomber.

By Round Six Louis is up four rounds to two, but Bowe is coming back into the fight. Having adjusted to Louis' mid-range attacks he either stays out of striking distance or gets right up close and personal.

During Round Seven Bowe steps back into range just as Louis fires a left jab and follows it up with an overhand right that shakes Bowe up. A further three punches from Louis and Bowe is forced to take a knee.

With the count at nine he rises, milking the allocated time, but Louis is on him like white on rice, throwing left hooks, right crosses and some fast uppercuts that Bowe just can't seem to avoid. He's hanging on, trying to make the bell, but with thirty seconds to go Louis is a man possessed. Sensing his best chance, he pounces. With another belting right he sends Bowe sinking to the floor.

The ref starts the count but one look at Bowe's glazed-over expression says it all and the fight is waved off.

Verdict: KO win to Louis in Round Seven.

Sonny Liston vs. Floyd Patterson

This fight happened twice and, sadly for Patterson, ended in brutal first-round knockouts both times.

Verdict: TKO win to Liston in Round One.

Jack Johnson vs. Ken Norton

Johnson just can't throw enough punches or hit hard enough to worry Norton, who will outmuscle and outland Johnson.

Verdict: Decision win to Norton.

Gene Tunney vs. Joe Frazier

Tunney has the speed and skills to avoid Frazier, but not for twelve rounds. A ferocious, relentless Frazier will inevitably get close and work over Tunney's body with brutal shots, followed by hooks to the head.

Verdict: TKO win to Frazier in Round Ten.

Larry Holmes vs. Rocky Marciano

Even though Holmes won't have the power to hurt or keep Marciano off him, he does have the boxing skills, size and speed to control the twelve rounds and make it a frustrating night for the Brockton Bomber.

The Rock will have his moments and possibly score a knockdown but will find it tough to corner or hurt his opponent and will eat all manner of shots while attempting to do so.

Verdict: Unanimous Decision to Holmes.

Muhammad Ali vs. Jim Jeffries

Ali is too big, too fast and too skilful to even get hit. This will be a one-sided massacre.

Verdict: TKO win to Ali in Round Nine.

Wladimir Klitschko vs. Evander Holyfield

Here we have an interesting fight between two warriors of the game. Both are blessed with excellent technical skills and ring IQ. Holyfield is slightly faster with the better chin and stamina, while Klitschko hits much harder and is the bigger man.

In past fights Holyfield has struggled with tall jabbers like Holmes and Foreman, and unfortunately for the Real Deal, Dr Steelhammer has a sledgehammer jab and about four inches in height and four inches in reach on him. Combined with the fact that Klitschko likes to box tall, it will be a very tricky and difficult fight for the American to win.

The Ukrainian will have a disciplined approach, relying on his jab and right to continually reset his opponent. Klitschko will keep the volume of punches to a minimum and not open up too much, limiting Holyfield's opportunities at countering. A cagey and pretty anticlimactic affair will see Klitschko to a comfortable points win.

Verdict: Decision win to W. Klitschko.

Jack Dempsey vs. Max Schmeling

If Schmeling can settle into his stride and start unloading with the overhand right, he could very well beat Dempsey in a long, hard fight. However, will Dempsey give Schmeling the opportunity? I very much doubt it.

Once the bell goes, the Manassa Mauler comes out like a tornado, completely overwhelming the German and blitzing him with rights and lefts that continually find their mark. A pulverising three rounds see Schmeling taken out with a fast and powerful right to the jaw.

Verdict: KO win to Dempsey in Round Three.

Co-main Event: Vitali Klitschko vs. George Foreman

The immovable object meets the unstoppable force; a clash of two big, tough dudes from either side of the Atlantic.

Neither fighter takes a backwards step and both are come-forward, aggressive power punchers. You have the most durable chin almost cast from iron against the strongest and most powerful puncher. If this were a video game their power and chin stats would be completely maxed out.

Will Foreman's punches have any effect on Klitschko's mandible? Or will the Ukrainian withstand the punishment and finish off Big

George in the latter rounds? A difficult fight to predict that could go either way.

Physically, Klitschko is about four inches taller, thirty pounds heavier and has one more inch in reach. In terms of power, both hit extremely hard. With eighty-seven and eighty-four percent KO ratios, respectively, someone's getting put to sleep.

Speed favours Foreman, while chin obviously goes to Klitschko, as well as heart and stamina. Ring IQ is close: even though Foreman is excellent at cutting off the ring and forcing opponents to fight to his strengths, Klitschko is an awesome ring general and rarely loses rounds, so there is not much in it.

Once the formalities are complete the bell sounds and both come marching to the centre of the ring and start throwing bombs. Neither is giving an inch. Klitschko is establishing his jab and following it up with hard rights.

Meanwhile Foreman is landing some good, thudding blows to his foe's chin that open up a small cut over the left eye. One minute in and blood is already starting to trickle down the Ukrainian's face. The sight of crimson accelerates Foreman's attacks, and he throws some spiteful left hooks and right crosses that all seem to land.

Klitschko is taken aback by the sheer force of the blows and is struggling to avoid them. Foreman is a man possessed, tearing through Klitschko's guard and causing some serious damage. The cut has opened up further and blood has now started to flow from Klitschko's nose.

The round ends with Foreman dominating but having exerted a lot of energy.

Foreman had the most trouble with movers who countered his punches and tired him out. Klitschko is too big, too slow and too robotic to employ such a strategy; his only option is to ride out the storm and take out a tired Foreman.

Round Two and Foreman is again on top, landing hard and clean shots against the huge target in front of him. Klitschko lands some good rights but just doesn't have the punch selection to truly worry the American. It also helps that Big George can see the punches coming and can block/parry effectively.

Klitschko steps into range and walks straight into an almighty left hook. Sweat and blood flies off his head as he tries to hold, but a crushing overhand right finds the target and he falls into the ropes.

Somehow the Ukrainian is still on his feet, and Foreman is momentarily stunned. Any other man would have long been on the floor. He rushes in with a bombardment of punches. Some miss but the few that land finally cause the giant to tumble to the floor.

Klitschko looks up, nodding to the ref while he counts. Once at seven he somehow finds the strength to continue. The bell sounds mercilessly for him.

In between rounds Klitschko is slowly recovering, however Big George is already breathing heavily. His corner begs him to slow things down and catch his breath. But before he can the minute is over and it's back to action.

As Foreman moves to the centre, Klitschko is still hurt but has the wherewithal to hold and lean on his foe. There is not much activity for the first ninety seconds, but with Foreman getting his wind back he starts throwing some menacing shots. Nothing too spectacular lands and the round ends.

Round Four and Klitschko has his legs back but his face is a mess. Two deep cuts over each eye, a broken nose and a closing left eye don't make for a pretty sight. Nevertheless, he doesn't even flinch when the corner addresses his wounds. A lot of hugging and not much punching happens in this round while both do their best to recover.

The fighters come out for the fifth and Klitschko opens up with some piston left jabs and hard rights.

Foreman has got his second wind and knows this is his best chance to end the fight. He starts letting rip with his heavy blows. It doesn't matter if it is his left or right that land. Whenever they do, Klitschko feels the power and towards the end of the round is stunned by another left hook. A hard right uppercut forces him to take a knee.

Once again, he beats the count, but Big George comes in like a tornado, landing another two-punch combo that sends the Ukrainian down for the third and final time. The ref has seen enough, and the fight is called off just in time as Foreman had literally emptied his tank.

Verdict: TKO win to Foreman in Round Five.

Main Event: Mike Tyson vs. Lennox Lewis

A fight of this magnitude isn't just big because of the names involved or the skills of the fighters; there is a decades-long history between the pair which began all the way back in 1983.

Lewis had just won the Junior World Championships and was promptly told he didn't beat America's best young fighter. So, as any brave warrior would do, Lewis and his trainer jumped in a car and went straight to Tyson's gym, where they sparred. An onlooking Cus actually proclaimed, "Mike! You're gonna meet him someday; don't you do that!"

Tyson tore up the division in the 1980s while Lewis stayed in the amateurs. By the time the Englishman's reputation began to grow in the 1990s, Tyson was incarcerated. In 1996 Tyson was ordered to face Lewis as a mandatory, however he opted to pay step aside money in the region of three million dollars so the long-awaited and admittedly bigger fight with Holyfield could be scheduled.

When they finally settled the score in 2002 Lewis was clearly the best fighter in the world and was in top form, dispatching Tyson in a one-sided beat down. However, we are here to assess how a prime Mike Tyson from the 1980s will do against a prime Lennox Lewis of the late 1990s, not the shot and clearly past his prime 2002 version of Iron Mike.

This isn't just a fight between two gladiators primed for combat, but also a clash between two of the greatest trainers. You have Cus D'Amato, the no-nonsense New Yorker who trained and guided three heavyweight fighters to the championship. He is facing off against Emanuel Steward, trainer of two of the greatest heavyweights in history Lennox Lewis and Wladimir Klitschko. A total of forty-one world champions have emanated from the Kronk Gym, a mind-blowing number and frankly a testament to Emmanuel's greatness.

With the fight date booked, Tyson was in the crowd watching with keen interest as George Foreman knocked out Lennox Lewis in five rounds during the last fight card. A delighted Mike couldn't help but gain confidence in the loss and while a dejected Lennox was being interviewed, Kid Dynamite stormed the ring and taunted Lewis over the demoralising loss.

The Brit's camp was livid and an all-out riot ensued with trainers, managers and security losing control while the two boxers were pulled apart but continued screaming obscenities at each other.

A genuine hatred and needle has flowed throughout the build up with both boxers declaring they will knock the other out viciously.

With the fans seated, a hush has entered the arena. The MC pumps up the crowd with an awesome introduction, bellowing, "Are you ready? Boxing fans from around the world, I said, are you ready?"

The fans go wild and roar their enthusiasm as commentators hype up the fight, claiming it embodies the rivalry between the USA and UK: you have the brash, outspoken, larger-than-life American against the calm, well-mannered, quintessential Englishman.

With both fighters in the ring the national anthems begin. While "God Save the Queen" echoes throughout the arena, the American fans remain respectful. The same can't be said about the Brits, with some booing the "Star-Spangled Banner".

The bell rings and Tyson comes storming out the gate looking to put a hurt on Lewis. He throws some quickfire jabs and hooks, landing a couple of hard shots to the body. Lewis is fully prepared for the early assault and continually ties up Tyson, holding when up close, leaning on him and throwing some quick uppercuts.

Once separated Tyson comes in bobbing and weaving, avoiding the jab and letting rip with a great right cross that glances off his foe's chin. Another three-punch combination from the American pushes Lewis back, who covers up. The bell sounds and it is a clear round to Tyson.

Round Two begins and Tyson again comes out looking to take Lewis' head off. A big right for Lewis lands and forces Tyson to hold.

While up close, Lewis is constantly holding down Tyson's head, connecting with some uppercuts, a real effective strategy against the smaller man. The ref has to warn Lewis over excessive holding. Heeding the warning, the Englishman eases up the clinching and Tyson is able to land some good shots, but nothing too devastating.

Round Three and while Lewis throws a jab, Tyson is able to slip under and lands a colossal ring that detonates on the Lion's chin. Lewis is groggy and Tyson lunges with no regard for defence and starts putting everything in his punches. His foe is too smart and just holds, trying to slow the pace down.

Once separated an enraged Kid Dynamite is looking to end things, but each time he gets up close is forced into a clinch. With frustration setting in Tyson wrestles Lewis and they both fall to the canvas. The ref steps in and orders them to tidy things up. Lewis has recovered enough to see out the round while not throwing much.

Rounds Four and Five again go to Tyson who's slowing but still landing the cleaner, more eye-catching blows. With all the spoiling and leaning from Lewis, Tyson is getting tired and in Round Six a big right from Lewis sends him into the ropes.

Each time Tyson gets in position, a hard left jab from Lewis takes him out of his rhythm and when up close Lewis throws a hard right uppercut that keeps finding its mark.

During Round Seven a pretty demoralised Tyson is eating too many shots, and a powerful uppercut floors him. He manages to beat the count but is weakening, while his opponent is just getting stronger.

Round Eight and with Emanuel Steward's insistence, Lewis comes out looking to end things. Tyson knows the task is too great but valiantly battles on. A heat-seeking right from Lewis finds its target and Tyson is finally out on his back.

The ref waves off the fight and once everything has settled both fighters embrace and bury the hatchet.

Verdict: KO win to Lewis in Round Eight.

FIGHT CARD EIGHTEEN

George Foreman vs. Jack Dempsey

Ken Norton vs. Sonny Liston

Joe Frazier vs. Floyd Patterson

Joe Louis vs. Jack Johnson

Rocky Marciano vs. Gene Tunney

Jim Jeffries vs. Riddick Bowe

Max Schmeling vs. Muhammad Ali

Evander Holyfield vs. Larry Holmes

Co-main Event: Lennox Lewis vs. Wladimir Klitschko

Main Event: Vitali Klitschko vs. Mike Tyson

George Foreman vs. Jack Dempsey

To say this fight will be exciting is an understatement. Everyone will be on the edge of their seats. Two of the most brutal, fierce and clinical finishers in history squaring off to see who's the meanest SOB; this ring is only big enough for one of them. The bookies are taking bets not on the possibility of a knockout, but the precise minute it will happen.

Physically, Dempsey is the smaller man by three inches in height, twenty pounds in weight and six inches in reach. All things considered, Big George does hit the harder of the two with a higher KO percentage (eighty-four to sixty-two percent) and is also the much stronger fighter with the better chin. However, speed, heart and stamina favour Dempsey, who will be relying on his fast and explosive punches to take out his foe.

Whenever Dempsey was fearful of his opponent, it spurred him on, bringing out a caged animal ready for utter destruction. In this fight you can guarantee Dempsey is fully aware of Foreman's ruthless power and finishing ability, so he would be in ultimate killer mode.

As the ring clears out both fighters stare menacingly at each other, not blinking and not giving anything away. Both have come into the fight with supreme confidence with one goal in mind: to take out the other as fast as possible. A long, technical affair this will not be.

To give their fighter extra motivation, Dempsey's manager has informed him his purse for the fight will only be paid if he wins, similar to when he annihilated Jess Willard. Not only does this motivate Dempsey, it royally pisses him off and he's either going to kill Foreman or die trying. With an air of anticipation amongst the fans, everyone is on tenterhooks.

The bell sounds and both fighters come striding to the centre. Dempsey is in no mood to mess around and starts throwing some fast, hard bombs that surprise Foreman. The speed and explosiveness of each punch can be felt when they land, even if it's on the gloves. Big George knows he can't make too many mistakes against such a dangerous fighter.

Dempsey is seeing red and while Foreman is throwing a jab, the Manassa Mauler connects with a crushing left hook that lands just under Foreman's right eye, exactly the same shot Dempsey broke Willard's orbital bone with.

Foreman is down and feeling the punch, easily one of the hardest he's ever been hit with. Luckily, he is able to shake it off and continue. Dempsey comes charging back in but Foreman is now just as pissed off and starts manhandling his foe, tying him up while he recovers.

Round Two and Foreman comes out with a tighter guard and starts walking down Dempsey, whenever they get up close, he either clinches or just pushes him back, something he's finding easy to do with the size and strength difference.

Each time Dempsey is forced back he's struggling to let off any power shots and his opponent is constantly forcing him to reset while also landing some thunderous shots of his own. The round goes to Foreman, who has fully recovered from the knockdown and is now establishing himself in the fight.

Round Three and Dempsey is starting to get frustrated. He can't land any clean power shots and seems to be on the end of Foreman's hard jabs. Even though he is avoiding most of the swinging shots coming his way, some are landing, and when they do, they hurt. This is another Foreman round, he's firmly in control and using his jab to nicely set up the right.

Round Four and Dempsey knows he can't take many more of these hard shots. He comes out like a bull, but Big George is ready and as soon as he sees an opening lands a disorientating left hook. Dempsey's not sure where he is and while he's trying to recover, an overhand right sends him crashing to the mat.

The ref doesn't even need to start the count. The fight is over.

Verdict: KO win to Foreman in Round Four.

Ken Norton vs. Sonny Liston

Norton will make it a little tricky for Liston for two or three rounds, but eventually Liston will connect and Norton just won't have the mandible to withstand such power.

Verdict: TKO win to Liston in Round Four.

Joe Frazier vs. Floyd Patterson

Patterson will try to box Frazier and stay on the outside, similar to Ali's strategy, but if Frazier is able to close the distance and land often and hard on Ali's chin, you can bet your last dollar he'll be landing that beautiful left hook on Patterson. When he does, it will be lights out for the Gentleman of Boxing.

Verdict: KO win to Frazier in Round Three.

Joe Louis vs. Jack Johnson

Johnson just doesn't have the power or work rate to keep a predatory Louis off him. Louis will come in supremely confident and land his blurring combinations, totally overwhelming Johnson and finally knocking him out early doors.

Verdict: TKO win to Louis in Round Five.

Rocky Marciano vs. Gene Tunney

A beautiful clash of styles between two similarly-sized heavyweights. You have the slick boxer with excellent movement, speed and ring IQ clashing with the come-forward, aggressive brawler with unlimited stamina, rock hard chin and two-fisted power.

Tunney is slightly taller by two inches, is a few pounds heavier and has a nine-inch reach advantage, something he will be utilising as much as possible.

The early rounds go to Tunney, who circles Marciano and peppers him with fast jabs and rights while skilfully avoiding the oncoming attacks, all while not lingering on the ropes for too long.

When they tie up Marciano is the stronger of the two and works over the body with some heavy and debilitating shots. The odd hook and overhand right lands on Tunney's chin but nothing too spectacular and he's able to see the shots coming.

By Round Six Tunney has won every round, but the relentless attacks to the body by his foe are starting to have a real effect, slowing him down and forcing him to keep his hands lower than he would prefer.

Between rounds Six and Eight the Rock is setting a blistering pace, constantly throwing hurtful lefts and rights to the body, his clear game plan from the outset.

With each round that passes Tunney is fading ever so slightly, and by Round Nine is struggling to avoid the rabid wolverine in front of him.

Round Ten and the Fighting Marine is gasping for air. With three broken ribs he is trying to make it to the end, relying on the early lead he built seeing him to victory. Marciano senses his opportunity and, when up close, feints with the left and lands a bulldozing Suzie Q that swiftly ends the fight.

Verdict: KO win to Marciano in Round Ten.

Jim Jeffries vs. Riddick Bowe

Bowe is too big, too skilled and hits too hard to have any issues dealing with Jeffries.

Verdict: TKO win to Bowe in Round Two.

Max Schmeling vs. Muhammad Ali

This is a bad matchup for Schmeling; Ali is just better than him in pretty much every department.

Verdict: TKO win to Ali in Round Seven.

Evander Holyfield vs. Larry Holmes

Two evenly-matched heavyweights that are known for their skills and slickness rather than pure punching power.

Looking at their fight in 1992, which was a decision victory to Holyfield, does actually tell us quite a bit about how a fight would have played out if Holmes was ten years younger. Even though Holyfield won the fight, it was by no means a dominant or convincing performance. Holmes made it difficult and was able to win a few rounds and box cleverly. At forty-two years old Holmes in defeat showed his greatness with an impressive performance.

So how will a fight between the two in their primes play out?

The only size advantage is with Holmes' longer reach by three inches. Their height and weight are virtually the same. Neither fighter hits hard enough to worry or even hurt the other and a lot of their stats – speed, chin, stamina and ring IQ – are dead even, with heart slightly favouring Holyfield and power slightly favouring Holmes.

The fight will begin with both trying to establish their jabs, with Holyfield trying to close the gap and land some hard shots on the inside. But Holmes' excellent footwork will keep him just out of distance.

Holyfield will have some moments throughout the fight and land some good eye-catching punches, but the Easton Assassin's jab and movement will be too much for the Real Deal. Down the stretch Holmes will always be ahead on the cards and is smart enough not to engage in unnecessary exchanges.

Verdict: Decision win to Holmes.

Co-main Event: Lennox Lewis vs. Wladimir Klitschko

Here we have two superheavyweights known for their safety-first approach, a hallmark of the great Emanuel Steward. The best fighter of the 1990s going up against the best fighter of the 2000s. Even though Klitschko was the lineal champion after Lewis retired, they never actually met in the ring.

So how will a fight between these two great warriors play out?

To avoid a conflict of interest Steward is not in the corner of either fighter and has refused to visit either training camp or advise during the lead up to the fight.

Klitschko is looking to gain revenge for what Lewis did to his brother and has vowed to come out aggressive and put Lewis away. Lewis has refused to bite, simply stating everything will be settled in the ring when there will be nowhere to hide.

Once the fight begins Klitschko comes out looking to establish his hard jab and throws a couple of solid rights. Nothing big connects and Lewis is able to start timing his foe, landing a hard right of his own towards the end of the first.

Klitschko's jab, hand speed and tight guard is proving to be tricky, but Lewis is in no hurry and works his jab into the fight, landing a few and following them up with a couple of hooks and a right cross. One of the punches that lands on the Ukrainian buckles his knees, yet he holds on.

Rounds Three to Five consist of Klitschko landing some good jabs, but he has felt the power of his foe and is fighting a little too cautiously. With each round that passes, Lewis is landing slightly more punches and starting to take over the fight.

Round Six and Lewis manages to wrestle his opponent into position and while holding his neck down lands a hard uppercut that snaps Dr Steelhammer's head back. Klitschko starts to back off but the Lion is a ruthless finisher. He hunts down his prey and throws a huge right that sends Klitschko into next week.

The ref starts his count but can clearly see Klitschko's blank expression and calls the fight off.

Verdict: KO win to Lewis in Round Six.

Main Event: Vitali Klitschko vs. Mike Tyson

After witnessing Tyson's three-round annihilation of his brother Wladimir, Klitschko has been eagerly awaiting the opportunity to exact revenge. Not only is he looking to dish out the same punishment to Tyson, but he's desperate to restore honour to the Klitschko name.

It also doesn't help that during the build-up to this fight Kid Dynamite called Klitschko "robotic, stiff and a lumbering idiot who will get put to sleep just like his baby brother". Tensions come to a head during the weigh-ins with Tyson's camp continuing the verbal assaults and Klitschko finally snapping with an all-out riot almost occurring had it not been for the extra security on hand.

A lot of spite and needle is in this fight and the thought of losing is unfathomable to either boxer.

Looking at the tale of the tape, the size difference is pretty profound. You have the tallest boxer in this league in Klitschko against the shortest fighter in Tyson. Tyson is giving up a massive nine inches in height, thirty pounds in weight and nine inches in reach. However, being the smaller man has never phased Tyson and he has honed a style of fighting perfectly attuned to his short, powerful stature.

Speed is heavily in favour of the American, as are boxing skills. Power is about even; though Klitschko has the higher KO ratio and is bigger, he did fight mostly low-calibre opposition. Klitschko has a stronger chin, having never hit the canvas in forty-seven fights. Heart and size both favour the Ukrainian with stamina and ring IQ dead even.

A real case of David versus Goliath, but this time instead of a slingshot David is packing TNT in each fist.

With both fighters in the ring, Tyson stares up, trying to intimate the bigger man. The Ukrainian just glares back, replaying the image of his brother getting knocked out. Each time he goes over the KO in his mind an extra bit of rage bubbles up inside him.

The bell sounds and Tyson comes thundering out, wasting no time with pleasantries or respect. He knows it's either kill or be killed and he's firing shots with real menace.

Klitschko is a little surprised at the ferocity and speed his opponent possesses and while trying to stay out of position and keep things at a distance with his jab, Tyson slips in and lands a hard left hook to the body, following it up with another left to the head and a right uppercut.

Klitschko is dazed and ties up his foe, but the ref splits them up and Tyson comes back in, throwing some blistering combinations. A string of three punches land and Klitschko is seeing stars.

Before he can recover, Kid Dynamite launches an atomic bomb of a left hook that detonates on the chin. Dr Ironfist falls backwards to the floor, the back of his head bouncing off the canvas sickeningly.

Tyson is celebrating, believing there is no way anyone could recover from such punishment, but in the corner of his eye Klitschko is slowly rising, shaking his head and is now well and truly pissed.

Once fighting resumes, Tyson comes in looking for the finish, but his opponent is too wily and keeps tying him up. The round ends, a clear ten-eight to the American.

In between rounds Klitschko's corner is urging him to take deep breaths and calm himself down, urging him not to take any unnecessary risks and to slowly wear down the smaller man. The bell sounds and Tyson comes out again, looking to end the fight.

Unbeknownst to him Klitschko has recovered and has made a couple of adjustments. The round consists of Klitschko constantly circling and using his jab to control the distance. Tyson is still able to bob and weave into range, and when up close fires some hard shots to the body, a nice large target he can't miss.

Klitschko is also landing some nice rights and jabs that are already starting to disrupt Tyson's flow. However, it is another clear round for Tyson due to activity and landing some flashy shots.

Rounds Three and Four go the same way, with Tyson closing the distance and landing some powerful body shots and following it up with the odd blow to the head. However, Klitschko's awkward style and constant movement is making it hard to land anything too meaningful, and it also doesn't help that every time Tyson is close enough, Klitschko seems to find the target with his sledgehammer right.

A cut has opened up over Klitschko's right eye from a Tyson left hook and blood is starting to affect his vision. Tyson is also feeling the effects of the hard rights, with his left eye closing. Whenever they tie up Klitschko's bulk is starting to sap the energy from Tyson's strong legs.

Into Round Five and having fought at such a blistering pace while absorbing huge blows is causing both fighters to slow. Tyson's shots are not as hard or fast as they were earlier in the fight, while Klitschko is still throwing with real venom. A tough round for Tyson, who eats too many clean punches and is starting to feel the fight has swayed against him.

In between rounds Klitschko's corner stopped the bleeding with a big blob of Vaseline and are hoping it doesn't reopen. Tyson's left eye is now fully closed and he's simply fighting on instinct. He comes out at the bell and goes for broke.

Klitschko keeps circling and when he sees his opening puts everything behind an overhand right that Tyson doesn't see coming. BOOM! Tyson is knocked down. His mouthpiece flies across the ring and it looks like it's over.

The ref is reluctant to wave the fight off until he is certain it is finished, but like the true Spartan that he is, Iron Mike gamely gathers himself and makes the count. Mouthpiece back in, he bites down and charges forward however Klitschko is prepared and within twenty seconds he lands two more hard punches and Tyson is down again.

This time the ref has seen enough and waves the fight off.

Verdict: TKO win to V. Klitschko in Round Six.

FIGHT CARD NINETEEN

Jack Dempsey vs. Mike Tyson

Ken Norton vs. Joe Louis

Floyd Patterson vs. Rocky Marciano

Jack Johnson vs. Jim Jeffries

Gene Tunney vs. Evander Holyfield

Riddick Bowe vs. Max Schmeling

Muhammad Ali vs. George Foreman

Larry Holmes vs. Lennox Lewis

Co-main Event: Sonny Liston vs. Joe Frazier

Main Event: Wladimir Klitschko vs. Vitali Klitschko

Jack Dempsey vs. Mike Tyson

So, we have finally made it to the last fight card of the book! One hundred and eighty fights have filled these pages, showcasing some epic tussles, and what a way to kick off the final ten fights.

In one corner you have the Manassa Mauler Jack Dempsey, renowned for his brutal punching power and explosiveness and aggressive fighting style. He's squaring off against Iron Mike Tyson, also famous for his fast, powerful combination punching and finishing ability. This fight has been dubbed "The Meanest meets the Baddest".

Neither fighter will take a backwards step and both will be looking to utterly destroy the other. Imagine a seriously pissed off Dempsey literally smashing Willard's face in – breaking his orbital bone, nose and ribs en route to one of the most one-sided violent beatdowns in boxing history – facing a rampaging Mike Tyson with only one goal in mind: to knock his opponent's nose right into the back of his head. This fight will be fast, ferocious and not for the faint of heart.

Comparing both boxers, Dempsey is taller by three inches and has two inches in reach but will be outweighed by about twenty-five pounds. Out of the two, both hit extremely hard, but I would give the slight edge to Tyson with his higher KO ratio (seventy-six percent to sixty-two percent) and extra muscle.

Tyson is probably the faster of the two, easily the better technical fighter and superior defensively. Their chins are about even, with heart and stamina in favour of Dempsey.

Iron Mike is bang up for this fight. Going up against his number one favourite fighter is a huge honour for the Brooklyn native.

As the ref gives the final instructions neither man takes their eyes off the other. The tension in the air could be cut with a knife. The fans, commentators and audience are collectively holding their breaths, waiting for the fireworks to go off.

The first bell sounds and both come charging forward like two pit bulls entering a dogfight. Dempsey wastes no time throwing a left jab and a right that lands hard on Tyson's chin. Tyson shakes off the blow but before he knows it another three punches come raining in and he's covering up.

Dempsey gets a little closer and Tyson clinches, outmuscling his smaller foe and surprising himself at the ease at which he can manhandle Dempsey. Once they break Kid Dynamite comes in, bobbing and weaving and slipping some fast jabs. He lands a left hook to the body that makes Dempsey wince.

Tyson senses the effect and follows it up with a quick jab and overhand right that connect. Dempsey staggers back and before he knows it a crushing left hook sends him flying back into the ropes as he bounces forward. Tyson lands a perfectly-timed right uppercut and Dempsey is down and seeing stars. He makes the count and holds for the final ten seconds to see out the round.

During the break Dempsey's corner is frantically working on their man, telling him to avoid trading and slow the fight down. Knowing their man is up against a bigger, stronger version of himself, the only strategy is to ride out the next three or four rounds and hope Tyson tires himself out. A tall task.

Dempsey doesn't listen; he only sees red and wants to return the favour. He's either going to take his opponent's head off or fall on his shield trying.

The bell rings and Dempsey has recovered enough to throw some spiteful shots. However, Tyson is just too skilled and easily blocks the shots. With his peek-a-boo style and fast feet Dempsey is struggling to land anything clean. It also doesn't help being the lighter of the two and being easily moved into unfavourable positions by Tyson.

Dempsey loads up on a right but misses wildly and Tyson detonates a sharp overhand right bang on Dempsey's temple. He's down again, a hard knockdown that he bravely rises from. But with his eyes glazed over and legs still like jelly, the ref calls it off.

Verdict: TKO win to Tyson in Round Two.

Ken Norton vs. Joe Louis

Norton will make it difficult for three or four rounds with his size and awkward style, but once the Brown Bomber gets his timing down, a sublime four-punch combination will put Norton away.

Verdict: TKO win to Louis in Round Five.

Floyd Patterson vs. Rocky Marciano

Patterson will have to be on his bike the entire fight, relying on his hand and foot speed to avoid Marciano's brutal attacks. He might elude the Rock for a few rounds but eventually will get pinned against the ropes, a powerful overhand right ending matters.

Verdict: KO win to Marciano in Round Six.

Jack Johnson vs. Jim Jeffries

This fight actually happened in 1910 in a purpose-built arena packed with eighteen thousand fans hoping to see the "Great White Hope" Jim Jeffries finally put an end to Johnson's dominance. Jeffries was six years retired and past his best, however even in his prime he lacked the skill and technique to deal with the defensive wizard that was Johnson.

Verdict: Decision win to Johnson.

Gene Tunney vs. Evander Holyfield

Tunney has great speed and movement and will make it frustrating for Holyfield, who would prefer a dust up, especially against the smaller man. But Tunney will have to be at his absolute best to outbox and outwork a prime Real Deal, who has no issues dealing with movers like Tillis, Dokes or even Tyson.

On balance Holyfield is just too big, too strong and too good a boxer to have any real problems with the Fighting Marine.

Verdict: Decision win to Holyfield.

Riddick Bowe vs. Max Schmeling

Again, Big Daddy Bowe is just too big, too skilled and hits too hard for Schmeling to have any success. Expect a one-sided beat down ending with a fairly early KO.

Verdict: KO win to Bowe in Round Six.

Muhammad Ali vs. George Foreman

Imagine if the *Rumble in the Jungle* never happened and Foremen went on to dominate the seventies. He would rightly be classed as the greatest heavyweight of all time. This kind of book wouldn't be necessary as everyone would point to Big George being the best.

As fate would have it, Ali was able to topple the unbeatable monster in an epic showdown in Zaire and solidify himself as the best fighter of the seventies. This fight was watched by an estimated one billion people around the world, and for good reason. Boxing was the number one sport globally, headlined by fan favourites like Ali, Frazier and Foreman, all not afraid of mixing it up with each other.

So even though the version of Muhammad Ali that beat Foreman wasn't in his prime, a younger Ali will be able to deliver a similar result, having faster feet and greater stamina.

An interesting fact is that Ali's strategy going into the fight was to stick and move, keeping Foreman out of range and peppering him with jabs and rights while dancing around the ring. After the first round Ali realised for every one step Foreman was taking, he was taking three, something Archie Moore had drilled into Big George, which made him a master at cutting off the ring. Ali knew he would be too tired by the sixth so switched strategies and devised the rope-a-dope literally mid-fight.

Verdict: KO win to Ali in Round Eight.

Larry Holmes vs. Lennox Lewis

A tough fight for both. Holmes is better technically, has faster hands and feet, a better chin and superior stamina, but Lewis is no slouch when it comes to boxing skills. He also hits much harder and is a lot bigger, outweighing Holmes by over thirty pounds and having a two-inch height and three-inch reach advantage.

The fight will be a very technical affair with Holmes generally controlling the pace and distance with his stiff jab. But once Lewis settles into the fight, his hard overhand right will shake up Holmes and cause him to retreat into his shell.

Lewis will use uppercuts on the inside and keep his own ramrod jab right in Holmes' face. A nip and tuck kind of fight but a couple of knockdowns to the Lion over the course of the twelve rounds will give him enough to get over the line.

Verdict: Decision win to Lewis.

Co-main Event: Sonny Liston vs. Joe Frazier

It is a real shame this fight never happened as both fighters were mixing it up around the same time. Liston's peak was in 1960 and

Frazier's in 1970, but Liston was still active and dangerous right up until 1970 when Frazier was the champ, so a fight between the two was a possibility.

Had they met around the late sixties, Frazier would have taken an ageing Liston into deep waters and either forced him to retire or knocked him out with a brutal left hook. However this fight is considering the buzzsaw that is the Sonny Liston who ran through the entire top ten and forced Floyd Patterson into a title shot, against a prime and ready Smokin' Joe coming off a career-defining win over Muhammad Ali. This will be one action-packed fight.

In terms of size Liston is the bigger man by about ten pounds, two inches in height and a massive ten inches in reach – absolutely mindblowing considering the relatively small height difference between them.

Liston hits the harder of the two and has the much sturdier set of whiskers, whereas Frazier excels in speed, heart, stamina and ring IQ. A tough fight to call.

So, when the two combatants finally meet will it be a back-and-forth contest or a one-sided domination?

Liston is fully aware of Frazier's tendency to start slow and therefore piles on the pressure early, using his ramrod jab to keep him at bay. Every time Frazier tries to come in, BANG! The jab hits the target, upsetting Frazier's rhythm.

During the first two rounds Liston scores a hard knockdown with a powerful right that Frazier doesn't see coming. Frazier beats the count but is feeling the effects and before he knows it Liston is pouring on the pressure, landing another one-two that sends him down again.

As expected, Frazier beats the count and demands the ref let things resume, which he does.

Rounds Three to Five are all in favour of Liston, who's using his jab and power to keep Frazier out of range. When up close he smartly engages the clinch and muscles his opponent around.

Frazier is finding success with the left hook but nothing too telling. Some tough attacks to the body give Liston something to think about, but in general he has managed to rack up a nice lead going into the sixth round.

The freight train that is Smokin' Joe is starting to gather steam. Noticing his foe's heavier breathing and slowing pace only drives him on. The bell rings and he jumps off his stool and burrows into Liston's chest, pushing him into the ropes and unleashing hard lefts and rights to the body as Liston tries to smother Frazier. A left hook bounces off his chin, sending him back into the ropes. A right from Frazier is blocked and Liston manages to tie up while gasping for air.

The ref breaks them up and Frazier comes forward but walks into a jab that staggers him. He shakes it off and pushes on. By the end of the round Frazier has thrown on average three punches to Liston's one and landed over half.

The Big Bear is feeling the pace and on his corner's insistence he slows down considerably during the next two rounds, constantly holding, pushing back and spoiling Frazier's work.

This doesn't affect Frazier too much. As the busier man he outworks and outlands his adversary easily. The fight has swung firmly in Frazier's favour and he can feel it.

Rounds Seven, Eight and Nine are all Joe Frazier. He's gaining in strength and forcing the action. Liston is slowly wilting under the constant body attacks and a gash has opened up under his right eye from a patented Frazier left hook.

By Round Ten a bruised Liston has managed to get his second wind and comes out behind the jab, keeping things as simple as possible. Fire the jab, throw the right and tie up easily, right? Well, not exactly. Frazier isn't slowing down and keeps slipping the jab and coming up with the left, somehow finding the target, much to Liston's annoyance.

During the halfway point of the round Frazier ducks in but walks straight into a Liston right uppercut that sends him down for the count. He manages to gather his senses and beat the count, but the Big Bear sees his opportunity and fires some perfectly-timed shots that put his opponent down once again.

Smokin' Joe is hanging in there, but another hard jab sends him down again for the third time and the ref has finally seen enough. The fight is over and both fighters embrace, showing their respect to the other.

Verdict: TKO win to Liston in Round Ten.

Main Event: Wladimir Klitschko vs. Vitali Klitschko

Here we are at the final fight – not just of this fight card, but the entire book. And what a main event we have! Two brothers colliding to see who the superior sibling is. A real Cain and Abel showdown.

Surprisingly both are on thirty-six points heading into the fight, so the winner will also place higher in the league. Had this fight happened it would easily have been the biggest heavyweight bust up since Lewis-Tyson and would have proven conclusively who the better fighter of the Klitschko era was.

Unfortunately for fans, the fight was never even close to materialising, with both Vitali and Wladimir promising their mother never to fight each other. Very understandable and commendable given the amount of money and legacy that would have been involved in such a fight.

Regardless of whoever wins this fight, both are a credit to their family, the sport and their country and have conducted themselves with the highest of class and respect during their careers, even when Shannon Briggs hilariously toppled Wlad off the paddleboard while screaming, "Let's go, champ!" (Video can be found on YouTube.)

So, with approval from their mother, both fighters have agreed to set foot in the ring and see once and for all who the greater Klitschko is. No two fighters in this book know each other better, having lived and trained together their whole lives. Both brothers are blood-lusted and will do everything in their power to be the victor.

Both fighters are behemoths and two of the tallest and heaviest fighters in this book. Vitali stands at a massive six feet seven inches, with his younger brother just an inch shorter. Vitali is also five pounds heavier, but has a shorter reach by one inch.

In terms of power, both are concussive punchers with barely anything between them. Wlad's right is the strongest punch either possess, but on balance Vitali can throw venom with both fists so it's about even in this department.

Speed favours the younger brother, who is a more fluid boxer with better movement compared to the stiff and robotic Vitali.

Here is the biggest difference: Wlad has a susceptible chin and is prone to getting hurt and knocked out, while his older brother has no such issue, with a chin forged from iron. In forty-seven fights he has never been knocked down or even seriously hurt.

Heart favours Vitali, stamina is about equal and ring IQ goes to Wlad, given his technical skills and footwork. Saying that, Vitali is an excellent ring general and controls the centre of the ring better than anyone.

With the Ukrainian national anthem complete, both brothers stare at each other, showing no emotion. They have only one goal in mind: to finally prove who the better man in the ring is.

The bell for Round One sounds and we are underway. Wlad comes out behind his jab, keeping his older brother at bay. Vitali bulldozes his way forward and eats a hard right flush on the chin. He merely blinks and continues throwing his own shots. None land and Wladimir is able to skilfully manoeuvre out of position. The round ends and goes to Wlad. A very cagey opener.

Rounds Two, Three and Four all go the same way. Dr Steelhammer is keeping a tight guard and pawing out his jab, following it up with swift rights. Whenever they get up close he ties up, taking advantage of Vitali's lack of inside game. Wlad has the perfect strategy and is nullifying Dr Ironfist's strengths.

Round Five and Vitali has started to wear down his foe with some tough shots to the body and the occasional blow that lands upstairs but doesn't cause too much damage. He fully expected such a game plan and is biding his time, waiting for the right moment to strike.

During the round he notices that Wlad is still boxing very cautiously, but on occasion tiredness is slowly setting in and every once in while he doesn't close guard tight enough or move out of range quick enough. Still, he isn't able to fully take advantage, but feels his punches are starting to have an effect.

Again, rounds Six to Eight are all Wlad, who's displaying some beautiful boxing and starting to open up a little more, landing some great combinations and eye-catching rights that keep finding the target.

Vitali is refusing to go down, but the shots are causing his knees to buckle more than he would like. Luckily for him, his younger brother is refusing to engage and prefers to keep the fight as safe as possible.

Round Nine and a cut has opened over Vitali's left eye. The blood is constantly dripping into his eye, annoying him. Wlad spots this and mercilessly targets the laceration with pulsating rights that keep bouncing off his brother.

Wladimir circles Vitali but stays on the ropes a little too long and a huge left hook from Dr Ironfist rocks him. Another right just misses and Wlad is forced to engage the clinch. The ref steps in and with ninety seconds still to go he is hanging on for dear life.

Vitali loads up a brutal right and BOOM! cracks Wlad on the chin. He's down for the count.

He valiantly gets up but with a minute to go Vitali is piling on the pressure, throwing a left hook, right cross and right uppercut, all the while Wlad is trying to escape. He staggers back but is pinned in the corner and another two-punch combination for the older Klitschko lands and Wlad is down again.

The ref starts the count. Wlad is struggling to get up, holding onto the ropes for support. He barely makes the count. The ref takes a close look but signals things to continue.

Less than thirty seconds remain in the round and Vitali knows this is the best chance he has to win the fight. Again, Wlad ties up and holds all the while his brother is wrestling to get free. The ref breaks them up and with ten seconds of the round left Vitali steps forward, but Wlad is holding his hands up close to his chin, hoping for the bell.

Five seconds to go and Vitali feints with the right and lands a colossal left hook that Wlad didn't see coming. He's down again and this time the ref has seen enough, just in time as his corner is also waving the towel, saving their man from any further punishment.

Verdict: KO win to V. Klitschko in Round Nine.

Awards

Before we look at the results, I've added one more thing. Below is a list of awards based on the previous 190 fights. In some categories it was difficult to narrow it down to one winner...

Fight of the League

With so many awesome fights this was a very difficult category to choose a winner for. I've narrowed it down to the most stand-out bust ups:

- Joe Louis vs. Sonny Liston
- Joe Frazier vs. Jack Dempsey
- Sonny Liston vs. Joe Frazier
- Jack Dempsey vs. Rocky Marciano
- Joe Frazier vs. Rocky Marciano

Most Devastating KO

George Foreman's one-round destruction of Floyd Patterson.

Biggest PPV Fight

Easily the main event of Fight Card Ten, which saw the Greatest Muhammad Ali cross paths with Iron Mike Tyson. Two mega personalities with crossover appeal really shone a light on the sport, with the whole world stopping to witness the biggest fight of all time.

Fighter Who Drew the Most at the Box Office

Coming in at number three is Joe Louis, with six main event fights and one co-main event feature.

The second biggest PPV star of the league is Rocky Marciano, with five main events and three co-mains. Very impressive.

The number one draw at the box office with eight main event appearances – easily the most of any fighter – and one co-main event fight is Iron Mike Tyson.

Performance of the League

This book is filled with outstanding performances, but the one that stands out the most is Muhammad Ali's complete dismantling of Mike Tyson. A flawless game plan executed on the night to perfection. Some would argue Ali had the fight won with his mind games long before they exchanged fisticuffs.

Most Exciting Fighter

With so many exciting fighters all mixing it up it's difficult to pick one, so I'll list three truly all-action, fan-friendly fighters who always bring it. Even when they are outgunned or behind in the fight, their *never give up* attitude is inspiring.

At number three is the Manassa Mauler Jack Dempsey, a formidable fighter who had pulsating contests with Marciano, Frazier and Holyfield.

Number two is the Real Deal Evander Holyfield, who had some epic fights with Frazier, Louis, Lewis, Tyson, Liston and Marciano. The Real Deal brought action, heart and entertainment.

Finally, you've probably guessed that our most exciting fighter in the league is Smokin' Joe Frazier. A boxer with the biggest heart and a relentless will to win, he was involved in some of the most enthralling and memorable fights.

Showing no fear against some supergiants, Frazier is total box office and even in defeat fights like his life depends on it, with epic fights against Holyfield, Dempsey, Louis, Holmes, Bowe, Liston and Marciano.

One thing you can bank on is Frazier never having a boring fight. An amazing fighter and a great addition to the book.

Final Ranking

So after nearly six months of writing, we have finally finished all 190 fights. This felt like a fifteen-round slugfest with Rocky Marciano. Let's analyse the results and declare a champion of champions.

As mentioned earlier, if two fighters finish on the same number of points, the winner of their fight will be placed higher. The scoring goes as such: three points for a win and zero points for a draw.

I would like to preface this by saying that all of these amazing boxers are phenomenal and even if they have a losing record (which some inevitably do), it by no means takes away from their achievements and greatness. There had to be winners and losers of each fight and having a losing record against nineteen other all-time great heavyweights in their prime is nothing to be ashamed of.

Finishing at number twenty with a record of one win and eighteen losses is the Gentleman of Boxing **Floyd Patterson**. He found it difficult to string together any wins, with his only victory coming over Jack Johnson. His main issue is a susceptible chin. With so many hard hitters in the book it was hard to place him as the favourite in any of the contests.

Coming in at nineteen with a record of one win and eighteen losses is the Boilermaker **Jim Jeffries**. Again, he struggled to amass any real number of wins, with the only one coming over Patterson. Jeffries is from an era when boxing was still evolving from the bare-knuckle days and even though he is a big, tough dude and fit fighter, he does lack real technical skills and defence.

Now at number eighteen with a record of two wins and seventeen losses is the Black Uhlan of the Rhine **Max Schmeling**. Even though he has one of the best wins on his official record with his defeat of Joe Louis, against all these other prime fighters he wasn't quite good enough. His only two wins were over Patterson and Jeffries. His slow speed, lack of power and being on the smaller side held him back from accumulating more wins in this league.

Number seventeen is the Galveston Giant **Jack Johnson**, with two wins and seventeen losses. A great defensive boxer who was ahead of his time, but this time was over a hundred years ago and boxing has evolved to such a degree that not only are fighters much bigger, but also more technically sound. With his lack of work rate and power he struggled, with his only wins being against Jeffries and Schmeling.

In at number sixteen with five wins and fourteen losses is the Black Hercules **Ken Norton**. A great fighter who has a very awkward style and the heart of a lion, Norton actually amassed some respectable wins in this league, the highlight being Gene Tunney.

The biggest issue he has is not having a strong chin. With so many power punchers in this book it is hard to place him as a favourite when up against them. Also, he already faced Ali, Foreman and Holmes and had a losing record, which has to be factored in. Nonetheless a tough and hard boxer who gave hell to a prime Larry Holmes, and across three fights with Muhammad Ali.

We are in the top fifteen and next in is the Manassa Mauler **Jack Dempsey** with six wins and thirteen losses. Dempsey was total box office in this book and was one of the stars. His all-action style gave us some great fights and highlight reel KOs. Six wins is nothing to look down upon, especially when you consider his hit list includes Frazier, Norton and Marciano.

Dempsey's two biggest issues are his lack of technical skills and being quite undersized at 188 pounds. This was not too big of an issue when he boxed in the 1920s, but he was just not big enough against the fighters that would follow in his footsteps. Either way, it has been spectacular to have such a fighter involved in the league and even losing efforts against the likes of Louis, Liston and Foreman were pulsating *fight of the night* contests.

Entering at number fourteen with six wins and thirteen losses is the Fighting Marine **Gene Tunney**. Even though Gene is highly skilled with excellent movement, by today's standards he is a small cruiserweight at 190 pounds. He managed six wins, with the highlight being a superb performance against Sonny Liston, outmanoeuvring and outboxing the bigger and stronger foe.

Unlucky thirteen is the Brockton Bomber **Rocky Marciano** with a record of seven wins and twelve losses. The Rock was involved in some exciting fights, with his best win in the book coming over Holyfield, as well as strong performances against Dempsey, Frazier and Liston.

Marciano's biggest issue is his lack of technical skills and size. In his era this wasn't too much of a problem, but against more skilled and often bigger men it was hard for him to rack up more wins. Still, thirteen is commendable for a fighter under six feet tall and 190 pounds.

Finishing at number twelve is the Real Deal **Evander Holyfield**. Now we are entering into winning records, with Holyfield putting together ten wins and nine losses. Again, very respectable and even in defeat he made a strong case with excellent showings against Ali, Bowe, Marciano and W. Klitschko. More impressive were the wins he was able to notch up against Tunney, Dempsey, Tyson, Liston and V. Klitschko all falling victim. Holyfield was easily one of the most exciting fighters in this book and put together some truly remarkable performances.

Just missing out on the top ten is Holyfield's arch nemesis Big Daddy **Riddick Bowe**. He managed to collate eleven wins and eight losses, and to be honest, out of all the fighters in the book Bowe was the most difficult to place given his resume's lack of depth. Even so, a winning record is very respectable. His best wins were against Marciano and the Klitschko brothers, with two close fights against Tyson and Lewis. Bowe performed courageously and was a great addition to the league.

Now entering the top ten is the Easton Assassin **Larry Holmes**. Holmes put together eleven wins and eight losses, with big victories coming over Holyfield, Dempsey, Bowe, Marciano and V. Klitschko – an impressive line-up. Also, in defeat he displayed his excellent fighting skills with tough close losses to Lewis, W. Klitschko, Liston and Tyson.

Number nine is Smokin' **Joe Frazier**, a fantastic addition to the book with his fan-friendly, all-action style and heart of a lion. Holmes, Bowe and Frazier are all tied on thirty-three points, with Frazier having wins against Bowe and Holmes placing him higher.

Frazier has eleven wins and eight losses, with big wins over Holyfield, Louis, Holmes, Bowe and Marciano. Always fighting like a man possessed, Frazier showed tremendous heart in losses to Dempsey, Ali, Liston and the Klitschko brothers. Frazier's biggest issue is his chin, being slightly undersized and starting slow in fights against some murderous punchers like V. Klitschko, Tyson and Lewis.

Finishing in eighth place is the Brown Bomber **Joe Louis**. In terms of achievements, Louis is right at the top, but head-to-head against other elite heavyweights he comes up just a little short. This is still a tremendous achievement given Louis' prime was in the late 1930s, with the remaining fighters all being active in the last fifty years.

He managed to collate twelve wins and only seven losses, with some big wins over Holyfield, Foreman, Dempsey, Holmes, Bowe and Marciano – a real murderer's row. Even in defeat Louis fought valiantly with close fights against Ali, Frazier, Tyson and both Klitschko brothers. It was a real honour to have him featured in the book.

Lucky number seven is Dr Steelhammer **Wladimir Klitschko**, with twelve wins and seven losses. Again, an excellent performance and to notch up so many wins is a testament to how great a fighter he is. Superb wins over Holyfield, Dempsey, Frazier, Louis, Holmes and Marciano demonstrate what a formidable boxer he is. Even in losing efforts, Wlad did himself proud with tough fights against his brother Vitali, Ali and Bowe showing his class and heart.

Coming in at number six is Iron **Mike Tyson**. The baddest man on the planet put together an impressive thirteen wins with only six defeats including breathtaking wins over some formidable opposition like Dempsey, Frazier, Louis, Holmes, Bowe, Marciano and W. Klitschko. Even in defeat Tyson proved how tough a fighter he is with great showings against Ali, Liston, V. Klitschko and Foreman. Kid Dynamite is a truly special fighter and finished on the same number of points as the next fighter, but lost their head-to-head, resulting in just missing out on the top five.

So, our top five fighters in the league are now set.

Finishing fifth is Dr Ironfist **Vitali Klitschko**. With an impressive thirteen wins and six losses, the Ukrainian Terminator is a brilliant addition with big wins over Dempsey, Frazier, Louis, Tyson, Liston and his younger brother. Vitali proved to be one of the toughest fighters to beat with six losses all coming in tough, hard-fought fights. Klitschko could have finished higher if he managed to beat Lewis in a rematch or fought tougher competition during his career, something that wasn't entirely his fault. Either way, finishing in the top five is an outstanding achievement.

So, onto number four and with fourteen wins and five defeats we have the Big Bear **Sonny Liston**. An intimidating powerhouse with underrated boxing skills, Liston is a brutal effective fighter and a tough night's work for anyone. He has racked up quite the list of victims, with high-profile names such as Foreman, Louis, Holmes, Tyson, Bowe, Marciano and W. Klitschko. His losses were also finely contested against Holyfield, Tunney, Lewis and V. Klitschko.

The Big Bear was actually one of the pleasant surprises for me when researching the book. Coming in I never would have thought he would achieve such a high placing, but on balance I felt he was the favourite in the fights he won.

Entering our top three we have Big **George Foreman** with sixteen wins and three losses. This is absolutely remarkable, with his only defeats coming to Louis, Ali and Liston. Big George displayed his toughness, brutality and boxing prowess by literally smashing through sixteen other combatants, the only fighter in the list to amass sixteen knockouts, ending all his victories within the distance. A great fighter and if fate hadn't led to Foreman crossing paths with Ali, we could very well be claiming him to be the greatest fighter of all time.

Finishing runner up in position number two is the Greatest **Muhammad Ali**. Even though he has the same number of points as first place, he did lose in their head-to-head, so Ali just misses out on the top spot. Even then, to rack up an incredible eighteen wins and only one defeat against nineteen of the toughest heavyweights in history is superb, especially considering his only loss was a split decision that could have gone either way.

Just as in life, Ali exemplified what a boxer should be: courageous, upstanding and willing to take on all comers. A truly one-of-a-kind boxer and human being.

Please start the drum roll…

If you haven't already guessed, finishing in first place and crowned the undisputed best heavyweight in history is none other than the Lion **Lennox Lewis**!

With a super impressive eighteen wins and only one defeat, Lewis has shown his class against all manner of opponents, from knockout artists all the way down to technical masters. His only loss coming to a prime rampaging George Foreman is nothing to scoff at given Big George's stellar performance in this league.

In a rematch Lewis could very well have come up with a game plan to beat Foreman, but on balance I felt Foreman had the best style to overcome him. You could also argue that Ali only suffered one split decision loss whereas Lewis was knocked out, but given their head-to-head result it's only fair to give the title to Lennox Lewis.

Just as he did in his illustrious career, the Lion backed down from no challenger, constantly sought out the toughest competition and carried himself with class and dignity. A fantastic boxer and man who will be celebrated for decades to come.

Ladies and gentleman ... our champion: Lennox Lewis!

Final League Standings

		Wins	Losses	Draws	Points
1	Lennox Lewis	18	1		54
2	Muhammad Ali	18	1		54
3	George Foreman	16	3		48
4	Sonny Liston	14	5		42
5	Vitali Klitschko	13	6		39
6	Mike Tyson	13	6		39
7	Wladimir Klitschko	12	7		36
8	Joe Louis	12	7		36
9	Joe Frazier	11	8		33
10	Larry Holmes	11	8		33
11	Riddick Bowe	11	8		33
12	Evander Holyfield	10	9		30
13	Rocky Marciano	7	12		21
14	Gene Tunney	6	13		18

15	Jack Dempsey	6	13		18
16	Ken Norton	5	14		15
17	Jack Johnson	2	17		6
18	Max Schmeling	2	17		6
19	Jim Jeffries	1	18		3
20	Floyd Patterson	1	18		3

So, there you have it, folks. The bell has sounded for the final time and the crowd is slowly filing out of the arena. There's only one thing left to do: sign the rematch and let's get a sequel underway...

To stay up to date with all the goings on in boxing and to receive a free fight featuring Muhammad Ali vs. Oleksandr Usyk, please visit www.undisputed-boxing.co.uk and sign up to our newsletter.

Thank you for reading my book! I hope you enjoyed reading this as much as I did writing it. If you have time, it would mean a lot to me if you left a review on Amazon or Goodreads.

Talking about boxing is one of my favourite things, and I always welcome feedback and discussion about any of the fights in this book. Feel free to contact me at: bruce@undisputed-boxing.co.uk

Author bio

B orn in 1985, Bruce grew up on the mean streets of
Birmingham, England. He graduated with a business and
management degree from Aston University in 2006. At age twenty-
one he began working in the publishing industry and never looked
back.

At age twenty-five, the same month he put all his life savings into a
house, he quit his very secure full-time job and started his own
media company. Fast forward to the present and the company is
still going strong, with about forty employees, magazines across all
manner of sectors and events held in places like London, New York,
Dubai and Phuket.

Bruce still resides in Brum with his wife Sam, beautiful baby
daughter Mariya and two naughty cats, Princess and Coco.
Alongside avidly following boxing, during his spare time he loves
to travel, read and watch movies (especially horror). Bruce wanted
to include some awards here, but sadly he hasn't won any.

To contact him with any feedback email: bruce@undisputed-
boxing.co.uk

Made in the USA
Middletown, DE
26 February 2025